Bargello

A FRESH APPROACH TO FLORENTINE EMBROIDERY

Bargello

A FRESH APPROACH TO FLORENTINE EMBROIDERY

BRENDA DAY

GUILD OF MASTER CRAFTSMAN PUBLICATIONS

First published 2002 by
Guild of Master Craftsman Publications Ltd
Castle Place, 166 High Street,
Lewes, East Sussex BN7 1XU

Text © Brenda Day 2002
© in the work GMC Publications Ltd 2002
Photographs by Anthony Bailey, © GMC Publications Ltd, except as listed opposite
Drawings in text by John Yates; drawings in storyboards by Stephen Haynes
Needlework charts produced by Peter Rhodes

ISBN 1 86108 310 6

A catalogue record for this book is available from the British Library.

Edited by Stephen Haynes
Book and cover designed by Maggie Aldred
Set in Goudy Sans

Colour origination by Viscan Graphics (Singapore)
Printed in Hong Kong by Printing Express Ltd

This book is dedicated to my daughter Emma with my love.

ACKNOWLEDGEMENTS

My thanks are due to DMC Creative World Ltd, Framecraft, Macleod Craft Marketing, Christine Kingdom, Mary Jane Collection, Coats Crafts UK and The Craft Collection for their help in providing materials for the projects in this book; to John Yates for his clear diagrams, to Anthony Bailey and Sandra Oliver for their stunning photographs, to Peter Rhodes who worked with great patience on my original charts and to Maggie Aldred who designed the book. My greatest thanks must go to my editor, Stephen Haynes, who has shown patience over and above the call of duty on many occasions, and finally to my husband, Charles, who has supported me throughout the whole project.

MEASUREMENTS

Although care has been taken to ensure that the metric measurements are true and accurate, they are only conversions from imperial; they have been rounded up or down to the nearest whole millimetre, or to the nearest convenient equivalent in cases where the imperial measurements themselves are only approximate. When following the projects, use either the metric or the imperial measurements; do not mix units.

The exact size of the finished designs is dependent on the stitch count and the gauge of canvas used.

Additional photography: pp. 1–2 Sandra Oliver; p. 4 Whitworth Art Gallery, University of Manchester; p. 5 Parham Park, West Sussex; p. 6 top National Trust Photographic Library/Ian Shaw, bottom Lindy Dunlop; p. 7 Sandra Oliver; pp. 26–7 all architectural views Lindy Dunlop, except 27 bottom left Maggie Aldred; pp. 32–3 top right Maggie Aldred, bottom right Brenda Day, all other architectural views Lindy Dunlop; p. 44 top left Maggie Aldred; p. 44 top right, p. 45 top left and bottom right Stephen Haynes; p. 52 books Stephen Haynes; pp. 64–5 all water scenes Maggie Aldred; pp. 72–3 fireworks Haydn Day, buildings Maggie Aldred, others Stephen Haynes; p. 78 bottom left, p. 79 top right and bottom left GMC Publications/Chris Skarbon, other garden views Andrea Hargreaves; p. 86 top left Lindy Dunlop, bottom right Sandra Oliver, others Stephen Haynes; p. 87 top left Brenda Day, top right and bottom left Lindy Dunlop, centre left and right Stephen Haynes; p. 92 top left Lindy Dunlop, top right Maggie Aldred, bottom left and right Stephen Haynes; p. 93 left centre and bottom Stephen Haynes, bottom right Lindy Dunlop; p. 131 Adrian Huxley

Contents

PART 3: REFERENCE MATERIAL

Introduction

Bargello, Florentine, *punto fiamma* or flame stitch – call it what you may, this is a technique steeped in history.

From its gently undulating curves to its aggressive points, it makes a strong statement. Based (it is thought) on Hungarian stitch, many tales and legends surround it, for no one really knows how it evolved. General consensus has it that it was worked first of all in Hungary, not Italy.

A Hungarian princess married a son of the famous Medici family, bringing with her a beautifully embroidered trousseau. The embroidery came to the attention of the ladies of the Florentine court, influencing design in a centre which was already known for its high artistic standards. Flame motifs became the style of the time and were copied by the Florentines, who made the technique their own.

Another attempt to explain its origins suggests that it was Elizabeth of Hungary who invented this economical use of stitches, to be worked when there was a shortage of wool – although the majority of examples which I have seen were worked in silk, rather than wool.

Yet another version links the name Bargello with Princess Jadwiga of Hungary, who at the age of 13, married King Vladislav of Poland. To impress him with her skills, she worked, amongst other items, a bishop's cope, which included in its design the arms of both Poland and Hungary. King Vladislav's family name was Jagiello, and it is thought that over the years this became changed by word of mouth to *Bargello*, this name then being given to his wife's needlework.

Whether or not this is true, there can be no connection between the Jagiello family and the Bargello Palace in Florence. Begun around 1250, and at one time the residence of the *Podestà* (the chief magistrate of the Florentine republic), this building is now a National Museum. It houses a collection of seventeenth-century chairs covered in bargello work, but unfortunately there is no

Opposite page: Pincushion project featured on pages 74–7

Exterior of the Bargello Palace, Florence

direct link to the Palace, for these chairs were only purchased by the museum authorities in 1886. Though faded and worn, they are still a beautiful example of Florentine work. The colours seen today can only give a hint of their richness when first worked.

The Bargello Palace was at one time used as a prison, which gives rise to the penultimate version surrounding the technique. It has been suggested that while being held in the cells, the prisoners invented the technique of bargello stitch. The cells in question are below ground and natural light is very limited, making this explanation very unlikely. The invention of daylight bulbs was a long way off!

The final word on origin must go to Dr Paolo Peri of the Bargello Museum, who in a monograph on baroque textiles mentions that the stitch is reputed to have been brought to Perugia by Queen Gisella, the wife of St Stephen (*c.*969–1038), who in 1001 became King Stephen I of Hungary. Yet another possibility! The discussion still

Detail of one of the seventeenth-century embroidered chairs at the Bargello Palace

goes on – should Italy or Hungary take the credit for the introduction of this now famous technique?

Many museums and galleries around the world have examples of Florentine work in their collections. The Victoria and Albert Museum in London has several interesting examples, including a waistcoat front, English in origin and dating from 1840. The embroidered shape has been tacked out on fine single-thread canvas and worked in contrasting groups of colours: yellow, rust and dark brown contrasting with navy, dark blue and soft turquoise. Small areas of ivory define a very sophisticated colour scheme.

Courtyard of the Bargello Palace

A small pincushion worked by Martha Edlin in the 1660s shows the fineness of the canvas that was often used at this time. Shades of plum fading to coral, and navy fading to very pale blue, are stitched meticulously, and finished with a tiny cord piping in the colours of the embroidery. Backed with a pink silk fabric, this is a truly delightful piece.

As well as pincushions, bags, purses and personal items of clothing, Florentine work was also used for shoes, as an example in the V&A shows. Worked in England in 1720, in shades of pink and green silk and wool, in a basic zigzag pattern, this shoe – for the museum only has the one – would have been protected by a patten for outdoor wear. Finished with a band of double cross-stitch down the front, it gives us some idea of the intricacy and richness of costume in the eighteenth century. This, for obvious reasons, is a very rare survivor.

Florentine embroidery was also used for church vestments, such as the chasubles in

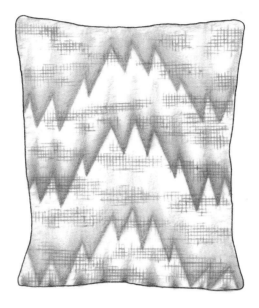

A sketch of Martha Edlin's pincushion, 1660s

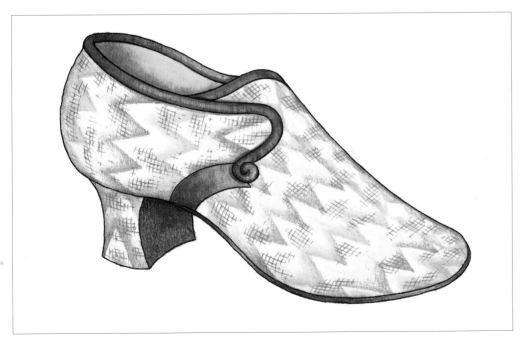

Bargello-work shoe, English, 1720

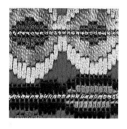

the V&A and in the Whitworth Art Gallery in Manchester. In the case of the latter, the two patterns which make up the design on the front of the chasuble have been very cleverly fitted to the shape of the garment – unlike some of the domestic pieces, where patterns for items such as chair seats were worked in continuous rows. There was no attempt to modify the pattern to relate more comfortably to the seat in question, and the effect is of pattern by the yard.

Parham Park in Sussex houses a fine collection of Florentine work from before 1800. Items from this period were often wall hangings or bed curtains, and the four-poster bed at Parham boasts a beautiful set of hangings, worked in narrow strips which were then assembled to make the complete item. Embroidered in silk and wool, each strip is joined by a narrow worked border of the same stitch, cleverly disguising the seams. How long this magnificent set took to complete one can only imagine, and one wonders how many pairs of hands were involved in the stitching.

The same thought comes to mind when one sees the dressing room at Chastleton in Gloucestershire, where not only the walls, but also the door are covered in panels of flame stitch – an awe-inspiring project, and a very rare one indeed.

The technique of Florentine work, which was found all over Europe, eventually found its way to the American colonies, taken there by immigrants across the Atlantic. There are several collections housing beautifully worked examples from before 1800, in which the colours of the yarns have hardly faded. They range from personal items such as purses – some with the owner's name worked as part of the design – to the

Eighteenth-century Italian chasuble in Florentine stitch
By courtesy of the Whitworth Art Gallery, University of Manchester

magnificent chair in the Metropolitan Museum of Art in New York. The whole of the front, seat cushion and sides of this chair are worked in Florentine stitch, but strangely enough the back is totally different in style and technique: it is embroidered in crewel wools, showing a landscape inhabited by animals and birds. One wonders whether the back of the chair was damaged at some time, and re-covered in a different style because of the difficulty of matching the original yarns. Perhaps one day someone will be able to throw some light on this puzzle.

American stitchers tended to give the various Florentine patterns names – such as 'Carnation' and 'Flickering Flame', to name just a couple – and this tendency carries on today. In the Glossary of Stitches at the end of this book (pages 108–127) I have avoided naming individual stitches, as I feel that it inhibits the stitcher. It is difficult to imagine a pattern called 'Carnation' being worked in anything other than colours associated with that particular flower.

In the projects in this book I have tried to combine Florentine embroidery with other techniques, because I feel that to isolate its beautiful patterns is to take a backward step. Embroidery should develop, not stand still. These patterns have great potential, as I hope some of the projects show, and by manipulating and developing them they can be brought up to date.

It is possible to let one pattern change gradually into something quite different, by altering the stitch lengths as I did in the Vibrant Pink Cushion project. The use of a variety of threads can give greater interest, and the addition of beads and ribbon extends this effect.

You will find, at intervals throughout the book, storyboards from which I have taken an idea, or in some cases several ideas, on which to base my designs. I regard this as a particularly important part of the design process, for only rarely does the design come from 'thin air'!

Embroidered bed hangings at Parham Park
From the collection at Parham Park, West Sussex, England

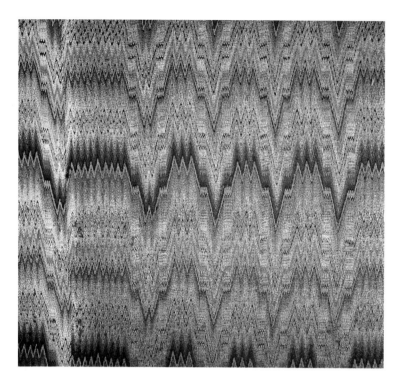

Try to build up a collection of cuttings from magazines and newspapers, postcards, scraps of fabric, feathers, shells and other ephemera, working with a theme in mind. This can take the form of a storyboard or, alternatively, a notebook into which you paste your finds, and from which you can draw inspiration. This avoids the 'blank paper' syndrome with which I am sure you are familiar. You might look for items where texture is important, or pattern, or you might, as I did, base each collection on a certain range of colours.

However you decide to assemble these collections, once you have a group of visual references, look at them in relation to the Florentine patterns. Perhaps the pattern on a shell relates to one of the stitches – could

The façade of Santa Maria Novella, one of the principal churches of Florence

this be developed into a design based on seashells, possibly for a cushion?

At this stage work some samples, on different sizes of canvas, adding beads and metallic thread if this is appropriate. It is important to scale the pattern used to the item in question – in other words, do not choose a very large repeat for a small project.

You may choose to draw your design directly onto the canvas, or you may be happier working in the first instance on graph paper, always remembering that the design on graph paper will be larger than the finished work. Whichever method you choose, start with something small, perhaps a greetings card, until you are familiar with the stitches, and then progress to a more ambitious project.

I trust that you will enjoy working through the designs in this collection, and maybe you will then feel inspired enough to work a design of your own. I hope you get as much pleasure from the book and its contents as I did designing and writing it.

One of the seventeenth-century embroidered chairs at the Bargello Palace

Materials and Equipment

For the technique used in this book, very little is needed in the way of equipment. As you progress and produce your own designs you will want to add to your collection of canvas sizes and threads. You will also need:

- selection of needles: tapestry, beading and sharps
- fine-pointed embroidery scissors
- dressmaker's scissors
- slate frame, or hand-held rectangular roller frame
- thimble
- ruler
- good-quality white tissue paper
- machine thread for finishing
- good-quality dressmaker's pins
- iron
- masking tape to bind edges of canvas.

FABRIC

Bargello embroidery is traditionally worked on canvas, which is a coarse, evenly woven fabric, usually made of cotton and stiffened with size to keep its shape. It can be bought by the yard or metre and is manufactured in a variety of widths and colours. It is available in a range of mesh sizes, which are determined by the number of holes to the inch (2.5cm).

Single-thread or *mono* canvas can be used, but I recommend that you choose instead *interlock* canvas, which is now available in a wide range of colours as well as the traditional white or natural.

Mono canvas

This is a single canvas which consists of an even grid of horizontal and vertical threads. It is loosely woven and frays easily, and can present problems during the blocking (stretching) process. This is because a stitch worked over only one thread of the canvas can move sideways under the single warp thread and spoil the design.

Interlock canvas

This has a single warp thread and two fine weft threads which interlock during the weaving process and so prevent any distortion or loss of small stitches, making it very suitable for bargello work.

EMBROIDERY THREADS

In the past, woollen, or very often silk, threads have been used, as they are hard-wearing and available in a wide range of colours. Today a much wider selection of threads is available, and experimentation beyond the traditional range can produce some interesting results. Anything which will go through the eye of the needle and the mesh of the canvas without distortion can be considered.

While the projects in this book have been worked using easily obtained threads, you might build up a collection of oddments

of fancy knitting yarns, crochet cotton, stranded cotton, metallic threads, raffia and ribbon. Group them together into categories – matt, shiny, fine and thick, smooth and textured – and use them creatively. The main criterion for choosing a thread will always be that particular thread's ability to cover the canvas adequately. Remember that fine threads can be doubled or added to, and that thick threads can sometimes be divided.

The following threads have been used in the projects, but there are many more which you might consider:

• **Stranded cotton** is normally available in 8m skeins in an extensive range of colours. It is a six-strand thread with a slight sheen and is very adaptable.
• **Perlé cotton** (coton perlé) is a two-ply thread which is more lustrous than stranded cotton and cannot be split. It comes in four sizes: 3, 5, 8 and 12 (no. 3 being the thickest). A metallic version is available in a limited range of colours.
• **Coton à broder** is a single thickness thread, softer than stranded or perlé cotton and not as lustrous. It is available in a range of sizes.
• **Soft embroidery cotton** is a single-thickness thread, available in a wide range of colours. It is soft to the touch, as its name suggests, with good covering qualities.
• **Caron Wildflowers** is a single-strand,

hand-dyed cotton, in variegated or space-dyed colours. The shading of these skeins is beautiful, making them particularly suitable for bargello work.
• **Metallic embroidery floss** is a six-strand thread which can be split in the same way as stranded cotton and is approximately the same weight.
• **Metallic braids** come in several widths. Experiment with them to find the one most suitable for your project.

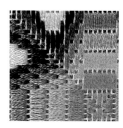

- **Blending filaments** are meant to be used in conjunction with other threads to give them added sparkle or lustre.
- **Narrow double-sided satin ribbon** is a useful addition to the list, but care must be taken not to twist it when stitching.
- **Crochet cotton** is a single-thickness thread, with a lustrous surface giving a smooth finish to the stitches. Because it is so tightly twisted it can present problems, and care should always be taken when using it in a design.
- **Tapestry wool**, which is loosely spun, is available in a wide range of colours which catch the light beautifully.
- **Crewel wool** is more highly spun and not so lustrous, but is very useful as it is multi-stranded, making it very versatile.

NEEDLES

There are many types of needles and each performs a slightly different function. Although they are, to some degree, interchangeable, it is advisable to use the appropriate needle for each task.

- **Tapestry needles** have a rounded point and a wide, easily threaded eye. Each stitch in bargello embroidery shares the same hole of the canvas with the matching stitch on the previous row, so a pointed needle would split the stitch and spoil the pattern. Tapestry needles are available in sizes 14 to 26, 14 being the largest. Packets of mixed sizes can be obtained, but you might find it more satisfactory to buy one-size packets of the most useful sizes: 18, 20, 22 and 24.

- **Sharps needles** are, as their name suggests, fine and sharp-pointed with a small eye. They are useful for general sewing tasks such as hemming, and come in sizes 3 to 10.
- **Beading needles** are very long and fine, and are used for attaching beads. They are available in sizes 10 to 13. For the projects in this book a size 10 is adequate, but if you find the beading needle awkward to handle, a size 10 crewel needle is a good alternative.

SCISSORS

You will need two pairs of scissors for the projects in this book: a small pair of embroidery scissors with very fine points for cutting threads, and a pair of dressmaker's scissors for cutting fabrics.

FRAMES

As the straight stitches of bargello work are not so likely to distort the canvas as, for example, half cross-stitch or tent stitch might, you do not necessarily have to work small projects in a frame. It *is* important to use a frame for larger pieces: firstly because this makes it easier to control the tension of the stitches over a large area, and secondly because the work is easier to handle in a rectangular frame.

The stitches are formed with two movements of the needle, going down through the canvas with one movement and then up from the back of the work with a second movement. You will find that it gives a neater finish if you can come up through an empty hole – that is, one which is not shared with another stitch – and down through a shared one. This way the previous row of stitches is not distorted.

There are two kinds of frames which are suitable for canvaswork: the traditional slate frame and the newer roller frame.

• The **slate frame** consists of a circular bar at each end, to which webbing is attached, and a flat bar at each side. These flat bars

have a series of holes at each end to allow for size adjustment, and slot into place through the rollers with split pins.

• The **roller frame** consists of a circular bar at each end, to which webbing has been attached, and side bars with slots in the ends into which the rollers fit. These side bars come in a variety of lengths, and are tightened with thumbscrews. Choose a length of side bar appropriate to the size of your canvas; any surplus can be rolled onto the rollers to tension it.

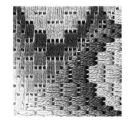

Do not use a circular or tambour frame; these are not suitable for canvaswork.

ADDITIONAL EQUIPMENT

If you stitch in a room that has poor daylight, or only have time to stitch in the evenings when it is dark, you might consider investing in a good-quality adjustable lamp. These are available from a number of different suppliers, and, if fitted with a daylight bulb, will enable you to see the colours of your threads in a more natural light.

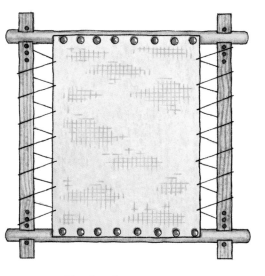

The slate frame in use

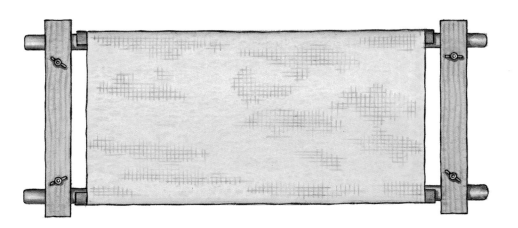

The roller frame

Basic Techniques

Before you begin work on your embroidery there are a few basic techniques with which you need to be familiar. Some of these guidelines will not be new to you, but others will help you produce a piece of work of which you can be proud.

PREPARING A STITCHING FRAME

A frame is essential when working on a large design, as it ensures that the stitching has a consistent, even tension.

Having cut your canvas to the required size, begin by folding over a 1/2in (1.25cm) turning at the top and bottom of your canvas. If the cut canvas is rectangular rather than square, make sure at this stage that you have it the correct way round.

Mark the centres of the folded edges, and the centre of the webbing on both rollers. With right sides together, match these

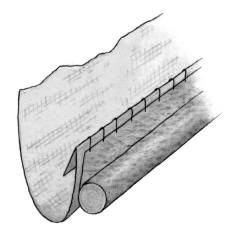

Attaching the canvas to the roller frame

points and pin the canvas and webbing together. Then, starting from the centre and working outwards, carefully stitch the canvas to the webbing, using small, even overcasting stitches.

Roll any surplus fabric onto the rollers. Slot in the side bars of the frame and tighten the screws to make the canvas taut. If your design is larger than the exposed area of canvas, it is advisable to trap a clean sheet of tissue paper between the layers of finished work as you complete an area and roll it on. This prevents any damage to the work.

Finally, bind the side edges of the canvas with masking tape, covering the cut ends of canvas which might otherwise snag and damage your embroidery threads.

PREPARING THE THREADS

While most of the threads you will use in the following projects are single-strand, there are some exceptions. Stranded cotton has six strands, which you will need to separate and reassemble to give greater coverage.

Locate the end of the thread in the skein and, holding the skein at the band, pull gently on the loose end of thread until you have the required length. It is better to work with a length of thread which measures no more than 18in (45cm), as pulling a longer length repeatedly through the canvas can spoil the surface of the thread. Now separate the strands of cotton. The best way to do this is to take the ends of the cut length in

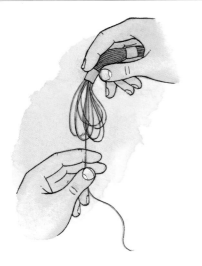

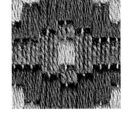

Separating and reassembling the threads

your fingers and gently pull apart. Separate each strand and then reassemble carefully.

The strands now form a looser bundle than before, and will therefore cover the canvas better.

THREADING THE NEEDLE
A needle threader is useful, though not essential; it may help when you come to thread the fine beading needle which you will need for some of the projects. To use it, pass the wire loop through the eye of the needle, place the thread through the loop and draw the wire back through the needle eye, taking the thread with it.

If you don't have a threader, loop the end of the thread around the needle and pull tightly. Slide the loop of thread off the needle, nipping it tightly between your fingers, and then push it through the eye of the needle.

Threading the needle with metallic thread can be difficult. Flatten the end of the thread

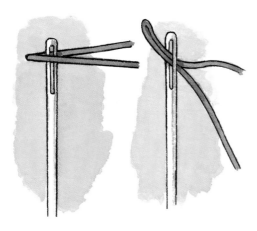

Creasing the thread helps it pass through the eye of the needle

A slip of paper helps in threading metallic threads

with a small piece of paper folded in half around it and push it carefully through the eye of the needle.

Alternatively, you could follow the manufacturer's recommendation and knot the metallic thread with a slipknot through the eye of the needle.

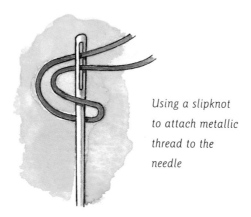

Using a slipknot to attach metallic thread to the needle

When you are ready to stitch, you must secure your thread to the canvas. Do not make a permanent knot on the back of the canvas – this would show as a bump when you stretch the finished work. Instead, anchor the thread with a waste knot. Knot the end of the thread and, leaving the thread on the front of the work, insert your needle into an area which will eventually be covered by stitching. Work an area of pattern until you reach the waste knot, cut it off, and complete the pattern. The thread which lies on the back of the work is now secured by the stitches of the pattern. Once you have worked a small area of pattern, you can join in a new length of thread in the same way, or you could darn the new thread through the back of the worked area, bringing it to the

front in the appropriate place. Finish a thread by darning it securely through the back of existing stitches.

SKILL LEVELS
For your guidance, I have indicated the level of skill required for each project. These should be interpreted as follows:

Level 1: suitable for beginners
Level 2: some experience needed
Level 3: further experience needed.

Finishing Techniques

This section will give you detailed information to enable you to finish your piece of work, on which you have spent many hours, in a professional way. The old maxim 'Don't spoil the ship for a ha'p'orth of tar' definitely applies here. It is such a pity to spoil a competent piece of stitching with shoddy finishing, so read this section carefully and finish up with a project that you can be proud to show.

BLOCKING THE FINISHED WORK

While some canvaswork stitches can distort the canvas, making it necessary to *block* or damp-stretch the finished piece of work, bargello stitches, because they are basically straight and run with the grain of the canvas, rarely need this treatment. But, should it be necessary, by following these instructions the canvas can soon be returned to its original shape.

You will need:

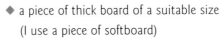

- ◆ a piece of thick board of a suitable size (I use a piece of softboard)
- ◆ several layers of blotting paper
- ◆ a top sheet with the outline of your embroidery drawn on it with a set square and a waterproof pen
- ◆ drawing pins (thumbtacks).

Place the blotting paper on the board and wet it thoroughly. Cover with the sheet of paper, finally placing your work right side

Blocking the finished work

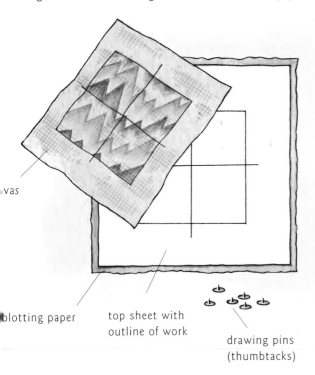

canvas

blotting paper

top sheet with outline of work

drawing pins (thumbtacks)

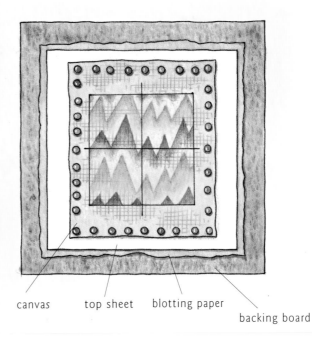

canvas   top sheet   blotting paper

backing board

uppermost on top of it. Starting from the centre of each side, pin the canvas to the board, making sure that the finished edge of the design lines up with the drawing on the paper. You may need to pull the canvas slightly to align it correctly.

Leave in a cool place until the canvas is dry, and then remove from the board. This process may take some time, but do not rush it.

STRETCHING AND MOUNTING

Unless you are experienced in this area, I would suggest that you take your finished project to a professional framer. However, if you feel that you are competent, then go ahead and stretch and mount the work yourself, following the instructions given in this section.

If you are stretching one of the larger finished projects, you will need to lace it over hardboard to keep it flat. For lacing you should allow a margin of surplus canvas at least 2in (5cm) wide, to take into account the tension of the lacing. If you have worked too close to the edge, then extend the canvas by machining strips of strong fabric along the edges. If the finished piece of work is to go into a mount before it is framed, you will need to take this into account when deciding on the size of the board.

Having acquired a piece of hardboard of a suitable size, mark the centre of each side, and do the same to the canvas. Lay the embroidery on top of the board, matching the centre marks, and, using drawing pins, pin into the thickness of the board, through the canvas. Working from the centre of each side, continue pinning at regular intervals

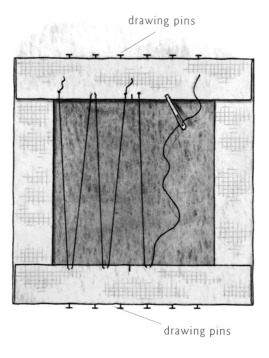

Lacing the first pair of edges together

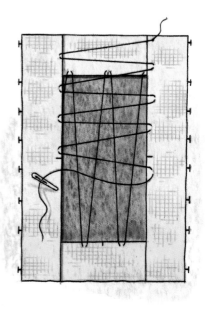

Lacing the second pair of edges

until you reach the corners. Using the weave of the canvas as a guide, check that your design is square with the board. Turn the board and canvas over. The embroidery is now face down. Fold the spare canvas over onto the back of the board and, using a sturdy needle and strong thread (I use buttonhole thread, doubled), fasten a long length of thread to the centre of one side.

Working from the centre to the left, lace from top to bottom as shown in the diagram. Repeat, starting in the centre again, but this time going from the centre to the right. Make sure that you have enough thread left for finishing. It is important to stitch well into the canvas at this point, to prevent the canvas fraying when it is finally put under tension. Having completed this stage of the lacing, remove the pins on the top and the bottom. Do not remove the side ones yet.

Starting from the centre, tighten each stitch in turn, moving the spare thread along from stitch to stitch, until you reach the sides. Fasten off the lacing thread carefully, cutting off any spare.

Now, working from side to side, complete the rest of the lacing in the same way.

You may mitre the corners of the canvas if you wish, but I find that it is sufficient just to fold them over neatly and secure with a few stitches.

MOUNTING INTO CARDS

Small pieces of canvaswork may be mounted into cards, making very acceptable greetings for family and friends. Suitable card mounts are readily available, and easy to use.

You will not need to block small pieces of canvaswork – just trim away any surplus canvas, leaving a small margin of unworked canvas which can be taped or glued in place on the card. Place the embroidery face up on a clean surface. Check that the design fits neatly within the cut-out of the card by placing this opened out on top of it. Remove the card, turn it over and run a fine line of glue or a strip of double-sided tape about ¼in (6mm) from the edge of the cut-out, on the wrong side. Turn the card over, and with the front facing you, lower it carefully onto the canvaswork. Press into place.

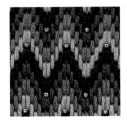

Mounting the work in a card

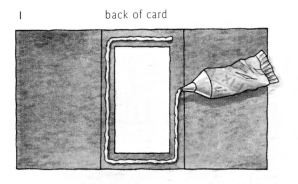

1   back of card

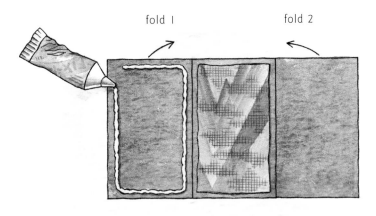

fold 1   fold 2

2   back of card

Place the card face down again and run a line of glue or tape just inside the four edges of the left-hand section. Fold this over onto the back of the canvaswork, and press into place.

MAKING A BASIC TASSEL

Cut a piece of cardboard the same depth as the required length of the skirt of your tassel. Decide how full you would like the skirt to be, and wind as many threads as necessary around the card. Loop a matching thread between the wound threads and the card, bring it up to the top of the card, pull up tightly and tie with a secure knot. Do not cut off the surplus thread, as this will be used to attach the tassel to your work.

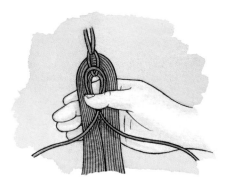

Use co-ordinating thread to bind the tassel

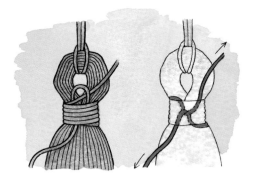

Binding the tassel

Forming the skirt of the tassel

At the bottom of the skirt, carefully cut the wound threads and remove the cardboard. Then, using a co-ordinating thread, make a loop as in the second drawing.

Bind the threads as tightly as possible around the waist of the skirt and knot the ends as shown.

Trim the bottom of the tassel so that the threads are all the same length, and attach to your finished work.

ADDING A CORD TRIM

If you are going to add a cord trim to your project, leave a small opening in the seam when sewing up. Cut the cord about 2in (5cm) longer than the required length. Bind each end of the cord with machine cotton to prevent it fraying.

Sew the cord on by hand, beginning at the opening, and tucking one end of the cord into this gap. Stitch in place by taking a small stitch through the cord and then a small stitch through the seam which you are covering. Continue in this way until the whole of the cord is stitched in place. Tuck the remaining end into the opening, laying it neatly alongside the first end. Sew the two ends in place, closing the opening at the same time.

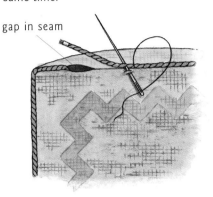

Attaching a cord trim

MAKING A TWISTED CORD

Instead of using a purchased cord, you might like to make your own, using one of the colours from your embroidery. Fine cords could be used to separate contrasting areas of bargello pattern within a design, providing yet another effect with which to experiment. Here is a basic method, which can be elaborated on by using a selection of threads.

Measure the required length, adding about 4in (10cm). Cut ten lengths of thread, each three times longer than this required length (for thicker cords add extra lengths). Put the lengths together carefully and knot as close to each end as possible.

If you are working on your own, find a handy hook, knob or window catch over which you can slip one knotted end. (Remember that you have to be able to

remove it later). Thread a pencil through the free end and, holding the pencil firmly to maintain tension, begin to twist, turning the pencil away from you in a clockwise direction. Continue until the thread is very tight and will not take any more twists.

Keeping the tension taut, take hold of the centre of the cord and bring the pencil to meet your first anchor point (the hook, etc.). If you are making a very long cord you may need the assistance of another person at this stage. Hold the ends together and let the cord twist back on itself evenly.

Having removed the cord from the hook, remove the pencil and bind both knotted ends together with a short length of machine cotton, then finally cut off the original knots.

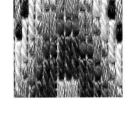

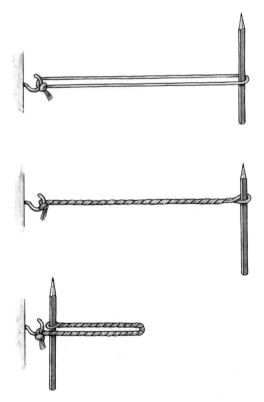

Stages in forming a twisted cord.

Kaleidoscope Coasters

MATERIALS

◆ white 18-count Zweigart canvas, 12in (30.5cm) square
◆ four Fabric Flair craft coasters
◆ size 24 tapestry needle
◆ roller frame of a suitable size
◆ eight 3⅜in (8.6cm) squares of medium-thickness card
◆ machine thread for stretching, or double-sided tape

THREADS

Anchor stranded cotton
I skein of each

A	B	C	D
342	253	1011	55
108	255	274	57
90	844	881	23
1030	846	882	869
213	1032	883	870
214	1033	884	871
215	1034		873
217	213		

STRANDS USED

Stranded cotton: 4 strands

These four coasters, each with a different colour scheme, are based on traditional bargello patterns. In each case a section of the pattern is taken and, by turning it through 90 degrees, patterns reminiscent of childhood kaleidoscopes are produced. This idea could be used to create a cushion, either by working on a larger scale or by repeating the same motif several times to fill the available area.

WORKING THE DESIGN

1 Attach the complete piece of canvas to the frame (see page 12).

2 Mark the centre by tacking two lines at right angles to each other.

3 Mark the centre of each resulting square lightly with a pencil.

4 Find the middle of each chart by using the centre marks, and mark each with a pencil.

5 Work one design in each quarter of the canvas. Four different colour schemes are shown, but you might like to try working all four designs using the same colourway.

6 Check for mistakes and loose ends, and remove your embroidery from the frame. It should not be necessary to block such small areas of stitching.

7 Cut along the tacked lines to separate the four units, and trim the surplus canvas to within ½in (1.25cm) of each design.

8 Take four pieces of card, trim if necessary to fit the coasters (allowing for the thickness of the embroidery wrapped over the edges of the card), and lace the

Coaster A

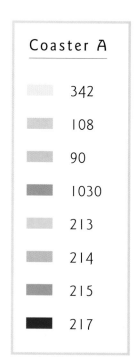

Coaster A	
	342
	108
	90
	1030
	213
	214
	215
	217

embroidery over the cards (see pages 16–17).
Alternatively, stick strips of double-sided tape close to
each edge of the card, taped side uppermost, centrally on
top of it. Peel off the tape backing and fold the spare
canvas over onto the tape. Press down firmly. Mitre the
corners to reduce any unnecessary thickness.

9 Place each mounted piece face down in the coaster.
Take the remaining four pieces of card, cut if necessary to
fit snugly, place on top of the inserted work and finally
push into place the translucent backs.

Coaster B

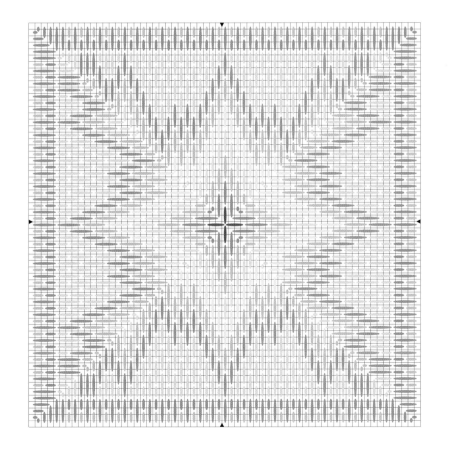

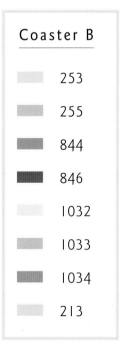

Coaster B

	253
	255
	844
	846
	1032
	1033
	1034
	213

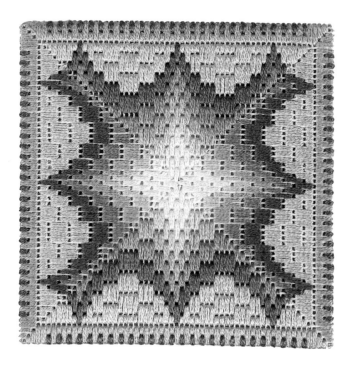

Coaster C

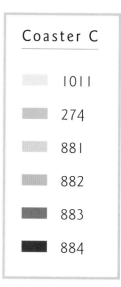

Coaster C

1011

274

881

882

883

884

Coaster D

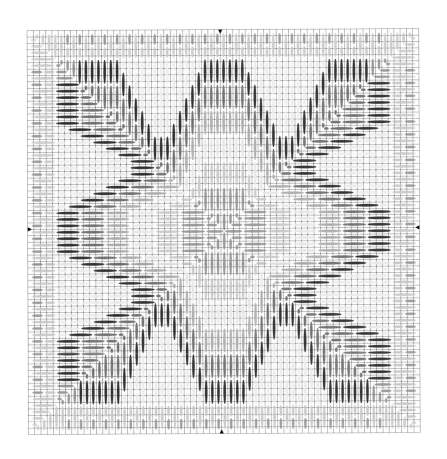

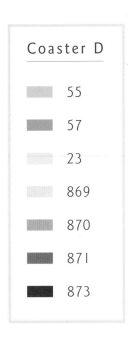

Coaster D

	55
	57
	23
	869
	870
	871
	873

Tiled Glasses Case

DESIGN SIZE: 3¾ x 7⅛in
                (9.5 x 18cm)
STITCH COUNT: 56 x 106

MATERIALS

- Antique 15-count Zweigart canvas:
  two pieces 7 x 10in (18 x 25.5cm)
- size 22 tapestry needle
- two co-ordinating pieces of fabric
  for the lining
- small roller frame of a suitable size
- machine cotton for finishing

THREADS

Paterna wool
I skein each of: 511 Verdigris,
701 Butterscotch, 643 Khaki

Anchor stranded cotton
I skein each of: 853, 884, 307, 326,
859, 309, 227

STRANDS USED

Paterna wool: 2 strands
Stranded cotton: 6 strands, used
double (this gives greater coverage
for an article which is to receive a
great deal of use)

*Decorative floor tiles and a piece
of ikat dyed silk were the inspiration
for this simple glasses case. The tile
patterns lend themselves to translating
into bargello work, and the use of
various colours for the infill of the
squares adds interest to the design.*

WORKING THE DESIGN

I Attach your canvas to the frame (see page 12).

2 Find the centre of the canvas by measuring in both directions, and mark
the centre lightly with a pencil.

3 Find the middle of the chart by using the centre marks, and mark with a
pencil.

4 Beginning from the centre of the design, work the olive-green diamonds,
followed by the gold ones, taking care to match the direction of the stitches
on the chart.

5 Work the olive-green border and the paler green infill next.

6 Fill the centres of the gold diamonds with 227 stranded.

7 Using the following sequence of colours, start at the top left of the
design and work from left to right, and then from right to left, filling in the
centres of the remaining diamonds: 853, 884, 307, 326, 859, 309.

8 Work the second panel to match.

9 Check for mistakes and loose ends, then remove your embroidery from the frame. It should not be necessary to block such a small piece of work.

10 Trim the surplus canvas to ½in (1.25cm), and turn under this allowance along the two long sides and the bottom. Mitre the corners of the ½in allowance.

11 Place the two panels together, wrong sides to the inside, and stitch by hand, using half cross-stitch or tent stitch, closely along two long sides and one end. Leave the top unstitched, and fold the spare canvas to the inside.

12 Cut two pieces of lining fabric 4½ x 8in (11.5 x 20.3cm). Stitch as the canvaswork, with right sides together. Trim the seams to ½in (1.25cm). Turn the unstitched edge over ½in (1.25cm) onto the wrong side of the stitched lining.

13 Insert the lining into the canvaswork pocket, hand-stitching from one side seam to the other, leaving the remainder of the edge open.

14 Cut three 78in (2m) lengths of 859. Following the instructions on page 19, make a cord.

15 Tuck one end of the cord between the lining and the canvaswork at the top edge, and stitch in place, following the seam, along the long sides and the bottom. Use one strand of 859 for this, and tie a knot when you reach the top edge. Cut off any surplus cord, tuck the knot inside the glasses case, between the canvaswork and the lining, and finally stitch the remainder of the top edge.

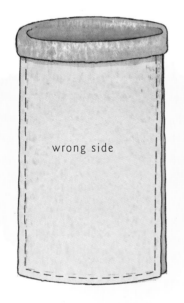

wrong side

Lining for the glasses case

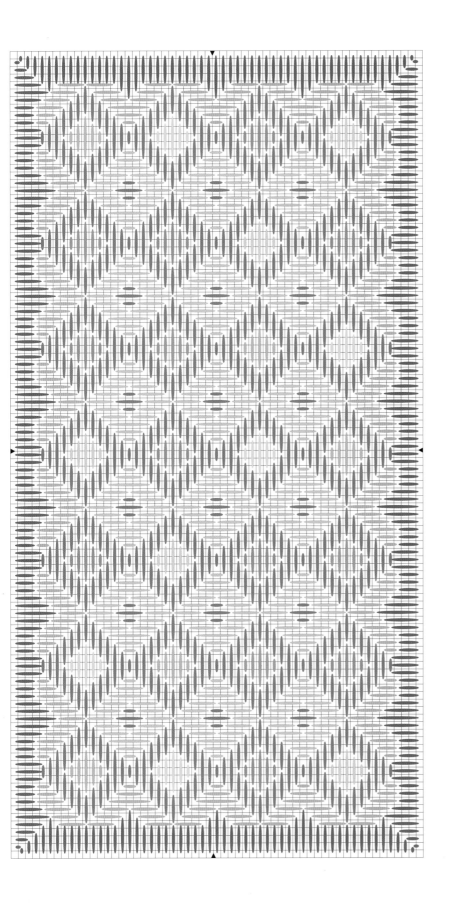

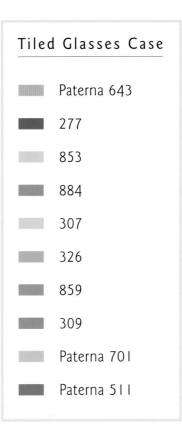

Tiled Glasses Case

- Paterna 643
- 277
- 853
- 884
- 307
- 326
- 859
- 309
- Paterna 701
- Paterna 511

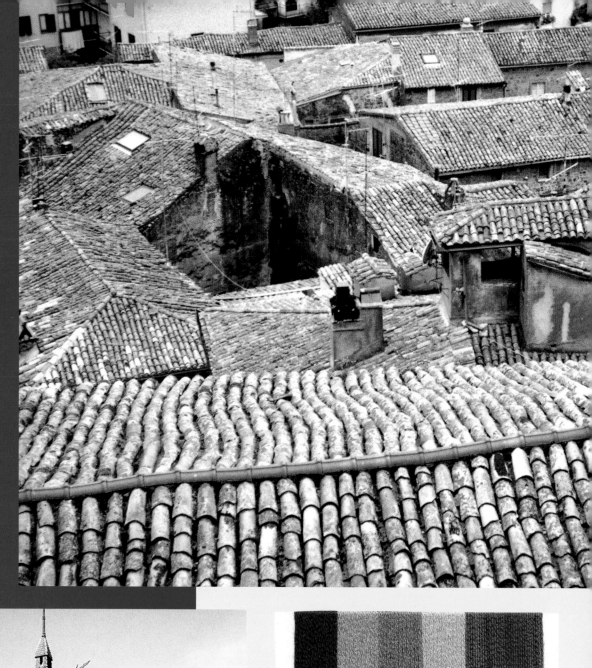

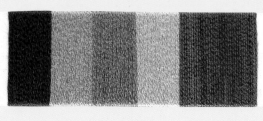

Place Mat and Napkin

SKILL LEVEL 3

DESIGN SIZE (WORKED AREA):
Place mat: 2 x 8¼in (5.1 x 21cm)
Napkin: 1⅜in (3.5cm) square

FINISHED SIZE:
Place mat: 15 x 11in (38 x 28cm)
Napkin: 13in (33cm) square

STITCH COUNT (WORKED AREA):
Place mat: 36 x 149 Napkin: 26 x 25

MATERIALS

- navy 18-count Zweigart Davosa:
  place mat 16½ x 12½in (42 x 32cm),
  napkin 14½in (37cm) square
- size 24 tapestry needle
- small roller frame of a suitable size
- thread for overstitching

THREADS

Anchor stranded cotton
1 skein each of: 129, 167, 1092, 142,
1089, 189, 150

Anchor stranded multicolour
1 skein 1345

STRANDS USED

Stranded cotton:
long stitch: 6 strands
backstitch: 3 strands
four-sided stitch: 2 strands

Glossy blue roof tiles, a beautiful Japanese pavement and sketches by Missoni for his exciting knitwear all inspired this place mat and napkin. Worked on an evenweave fabric instead of the usual canvas, the design has a very modern feel.

WORKING THE DESIGN

Place mat

1 Cut a 16½ x 12½in (42 x 32cm) piece of fabric for the place mat. Oversew the short sides, as Davosa frays very easily.

2 Attach the fabric to the frame (see page 12).

3 Work four-sided stitch 1½in (3.8cm) in from the edge to form a rectangle 13½ x 9½in (34.3 x 24cm). You might find it easier to work this stitch before you attach the fabric to the frame, to make measuring the rectangle easier.

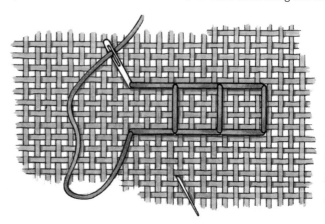

Four-sided stitch; see pages 105–6 for more detailed instructions

Place Mat

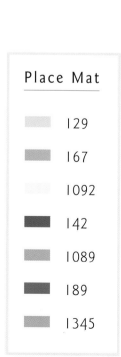

	129
	167
	1092
	142
	1089
	189
	1345

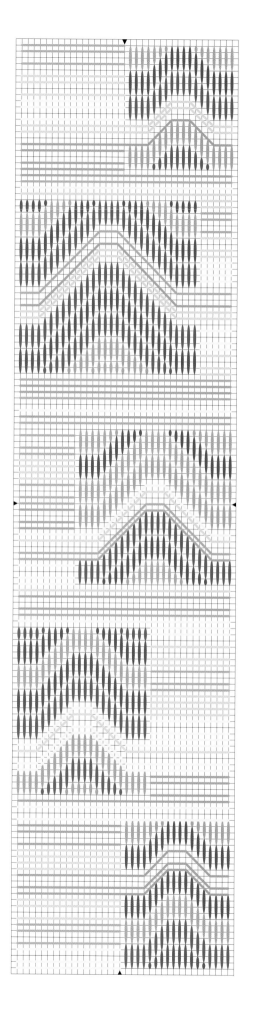

4 Count 9 threads in and 9 threads down from the inner, top right-hand corner of the stitching. Mark with a pin. This gives the position for the top right-hand corner of the embroidered panel.

5 Complete the stitching. Try to keep the tension even throughout, as the structure of Davosa is not as strong as canvas, and will easily open up if the thread is pulled too firmly.

6 Check for mistakes and loose ends, then remove your embroidery from the frame.

7 Place face down, cover with a cloth and press gently with a warm iron.

8 Trim the fabric outside the four-sided stitch to ¾in (2cm) on all four sides. Fray away the loose threads to form a fringe.

Napkin

1 Cut a 14½in (37cm) square of fabric for the napkin.

2 Follow the instructions for the place mat, stitching an 11½in (29.2cm) square in four-sided stitch.

3 Position the embroidered motif 9 x 9 threads in from the corner as before.

4 Complete the napkin to match the place mat.

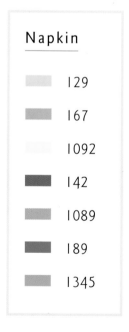

Napkin

- 129
- 167
- 1092
- 142
- 1089
- 189
- 1345

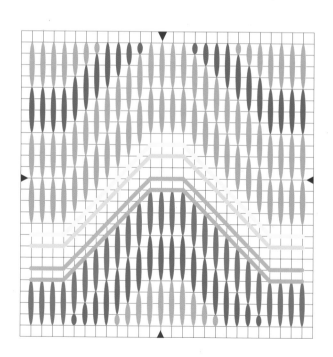

Napkin Rings

MATERIALS

◆ white 18-count Zweigart canvas, 8 x 4in (20.3 x 10.2cm) for each napkin ring
You might find it preferable to work several repeats of the design on one longer piece of canvas, remembering to allow enough spare canvas between the repeats to allow for finishing. Two napkin rings will take an 8in (20.3cm) square of canvas; six will take 8 x 18in (20.3 x 45.7cm).

◆ co-ordinating fabric for the lining
◆ size 22 tapestry needle
◆ small hand-held roller frame of a suitable size
◆ machine cotton for finishing

THREADS

Anchor stranded cotton
1 skein of each:
A: 341, 1045, 361, 336
B: 1045, 361, 888, 886

Caron Wildflowers
1 skein of each:
A: 052 Marigold, B: 137 Copper

STRANDS USED

Stranded cotton: 6 strands
Wildflowers: 2 strands

A textile design by Charles Rennie Mackintosh, and a view from a hotel window of terracotta roof tiles, provided the starting point for these napkin ring designs. Two colour schemes have been suggested, and the storyboard on pages 32–3 could provide several others.

WORKING THE DESIGN

1 Attach the longer edge of the canvas to the frame (see page 12), if you are working one or two napkin rings. If you choose to work as many as six, then the short edge of the canvas should be attached to the frame.

2 Find the centre of the canvas by measuring in both directions, and mark the centre with a pencil, lightly.

3 Find the middle of the chart by using the centre marks; mark with a pencil.

4 Begin stitching from the middle, working the design across the canvas, and stroking the stitches, where necessary, with a smooth nail tip to spread the threads. Complete the required number of units.

5 Check for mistakes and loose ends, then remove your embroidery from the frame. It should not be necessary to block such small areas of stitching.

6 Trim the spare canvas to ¼in (6mm) around each worked area. Cut one piece of lining fabric for each napkin ring, the same size as the canvas.

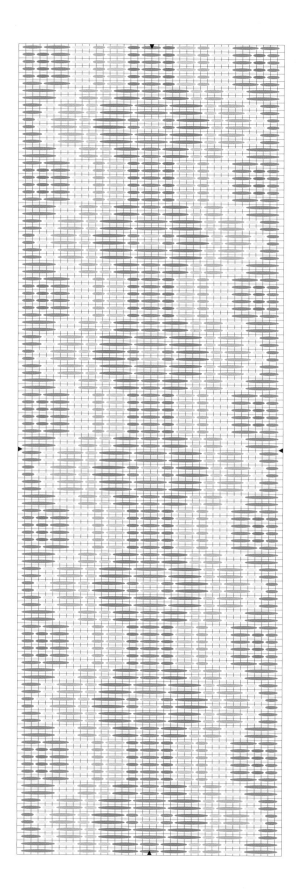

7 Put the canvaswork and the lining together with right sides facing. Machine or hand-stitch one long edge, stitching as close to the embroidery as possible. Press the seam towards the canvaswork. Open out flat.

8 With right side inside, match up the two short ends, and machine or hand-stitch across the canvas and the fabric.

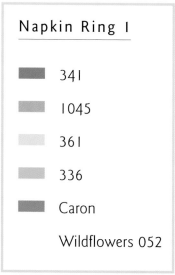

Napkin Ring I

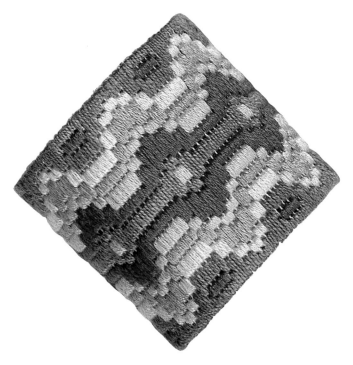

▬	341
▬	1045
▬	361
▬	336
▬	Caron
	Wildflowers 052

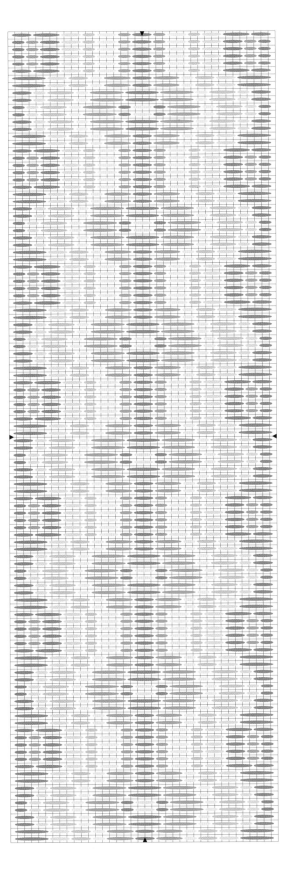

9 Turn to the right side and press this last seam flat, using the point of your iron.

10 Turn in the surplus canvas, match the fabric to it and hand-stitch the other long edge.

Napkin Ring 2

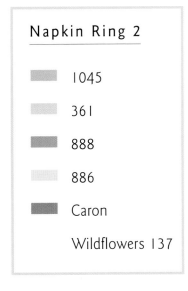

1045

361

888

886

Caron

Wildflowers 137

Bolster Cushion

MATERIALS

◆ red 14-count Zweigart canvas,
   14 x 16½in (35.5 x 42cm)
◆ co-ordinating fabric for the end
   panels
◆ two manufactured tassels
◆ size 22 tapestry needle
◆ rectangular frame or roller frame
   of suitable size
◆ machine cotton for finishing
◆ ready-made bolster roll, 16 x 6in
   (40.5 x 15.2cm)

THREADS

DMC stranded cotton
1 skein of 922
2 skeins each of: 154, 758, 152,
3802, 739, 150

DMC metallic stranded
5 skeins of 5282 Gold

Anchor pearl thread
2 skeins of Multicolour 1315

Caron Impressions
1 hank of MA052215 Marigold

(continued on page 48)

The richness of pattern and colour found in bird feathers formed the basis for this bolster cushion design. A ball of knitting yarn bought on a trip to Florence provided the colour scheme of rich raspberry, purple, soft pinks and gold – colours reminiscent of the medieval costumes seen during the many Tuscan festivals. The bargello patterns change in size to form the stylized feather shapes, the metallic thread adding extra sparkle.

WORKING THE DESIGN

1 Attach the shorter sides of the canvas to the frame in the usual way (see page 12).

2 Find the centre of the shorter side by measuring the canvas, and mark it with a pencil.

3 The centre of the chart is marked by a small black arrow.

4 Beginning at one end of the canvas, and 1in (2.5cm) away from the framed edge, work the half-motif as shown on the chart. You might find it easiest to work out from the centre of the design to each side; this will ensure that the pattern is placed centrally on the canvas.

YLI Corp. (USA) 4mm silk ribbon
2 metres of 70 Pink
I metre each of: 84 Damson, 23 Lilac,
86 Aubergine

DMC tapestry wool
3 skeins of 7107 Raspberry

COLOUR SEQUENCES (see step 6)

Cream: 739, 150, 1315, 86 ribbon
Grape: 3802, 758, Caron MA052215,
    84 ribbon
Purple: 154, Caron MA052215, 922,
    70 ribbon
Raspberry: 150, 154, 739, 23 ribbon
Pale pink: 152, 1315, 3802,
    70 ribbon

STRANDS USED

Stranded cotton: 6 strands
Ribbon: I thickness
Metallic stranded: Cross stitch
    edging 4 strands, centre line on
    units 6 strands
Pearl thread: I thickness
Caron Impressions: 2 strands

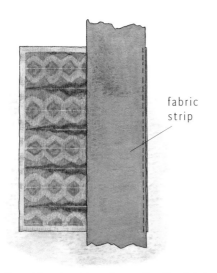

fabric
strip

Attaching the strips of co-ordinating fabric.

5 Follow this with the complete feather motifs, paying particular attention to the changing size of the stitches. The line of unworked canvas running through the centre of each feather shape should be worked in gold using 6 strands, over one thread of the canvas.

6 Consult the colour sequences given in the left-hand column if you are in any doubt. The colours are listed from the outside of the feather shape to the middle. The background should be worked in long stitch, using Raspberry wool 7107, and making sure that all the canvas is covered.

7 Complete the charted area, working one row of cross stitch, using 4 strands of gold, along each long side as indicated on the chart; position the cross stitch as close to the bargello section as possible. You will have noticed that there is a half-motif at each end of the main panel of stitching, which will link up and make a complete feather when you stitch up the cushion.

8 Check for mistakes and loose ends, then remove your embroidery from the frame. Block the finished piece (see pages 15–16).

9 Trim all surplus canvas to ½in (1.25cm).

10 Cut two 5 x 14½in (12.7 x 37cm) lengths of co-ordinating fabric. Place one long edge of the canvas and one long edge of one of the strips of fabric together with right sides facing. Tack and then stitch as close to the embroidery as possible, using a matching machine thread. Repeat at the other end.

11 Press the seams away from the embroidery.

12 Run two rows of gathering stitches along the remaining edge of the strips, ½in (1.25cm) away from the edge and ¼in (6mm) apart.

13 Pull up the gathering threads tightly and tie off securely, keeping the seam allowance to the wrong side.

14 With right sides facing, join the short sides of the fabric strips.

15 Turn the cushion to the right side.

16 Fold under one long edge of the canvas seam allowance, one canvas thread away from the worked area. Position over the remaining seam allowance, matching the pattern carefully. You may find this easier if you use pins to align the pattern.

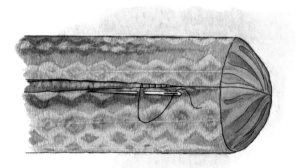

Closing the seam

17 Matching the threads to the chart, complete 1in (2.5cm) at each end of the long opening. You may find the first few stitches rather difficult, but persevere, as the finished result – which should be a virtually invisible seam – is well worth all the effort.

18 Insert the bolster pad, and complete the stitching, matching canvas threads and stitches carefully. Darn any remaining thread back through the canvas and under the stitching to secure it.

19 The two tassels were made from the following threads: 1 skein 7107 wool, 1 skein each of stranded: 3802, 3804, 154, 150, 902. Bind with the remaining gold thread. Follow the instructions for making a tassel on page 18, or use two purchased tassels instead. Sew in place centrally at either end of the cushion.

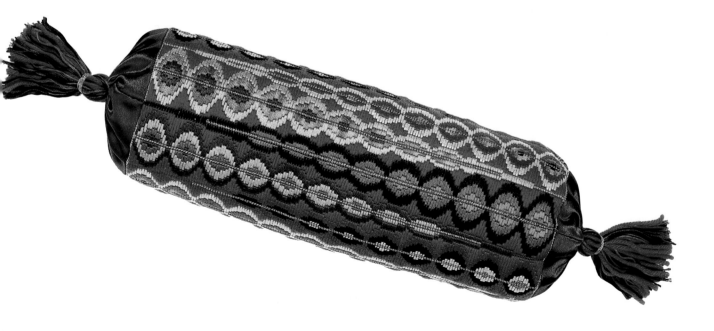

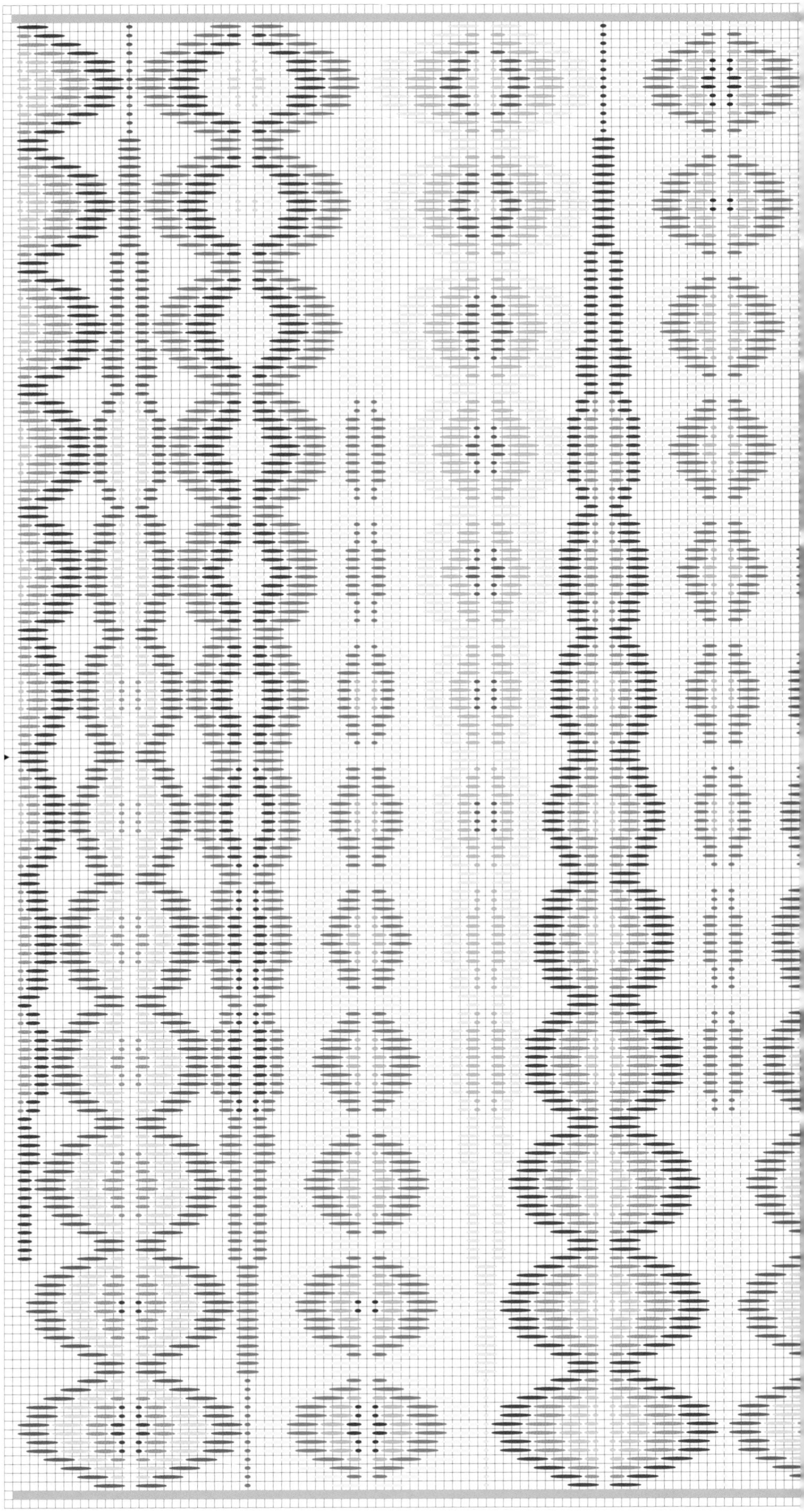

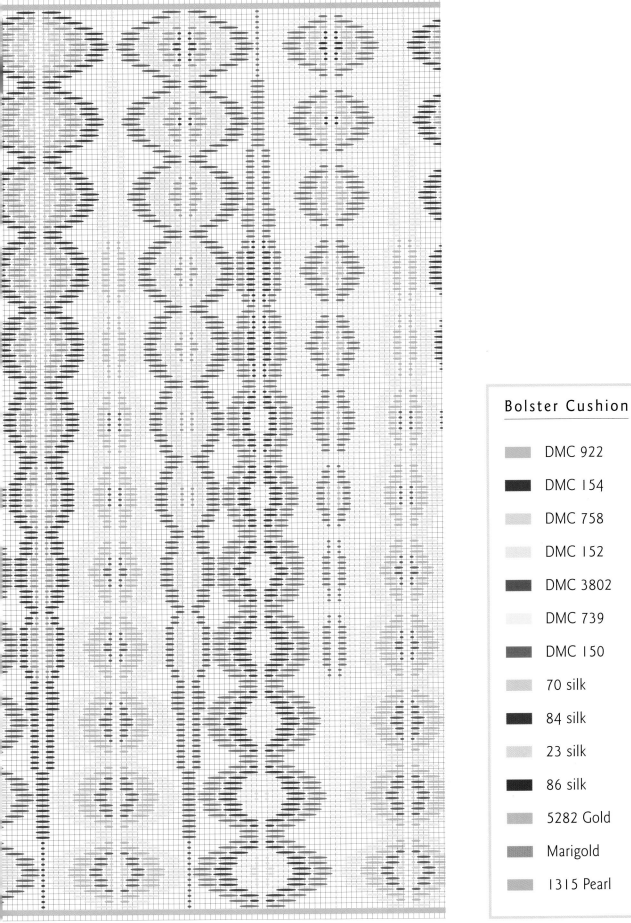

Bolster Cushion

- DMC 922
- DMC 154
- DMC 758
- DMC 152
- DMC 3802
- DMC 739
- DMC 150
- 70 silk
- 84 silk
- 23 silk
- 86 silk
- 5282 Gold
- Marigold
- 1315 Pearl

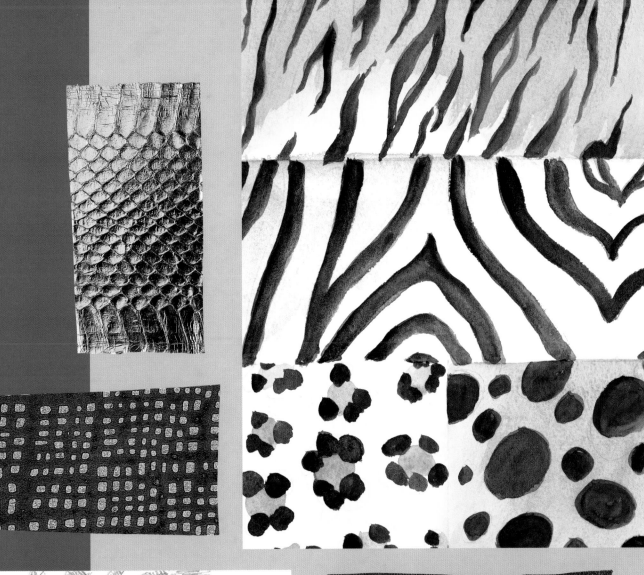
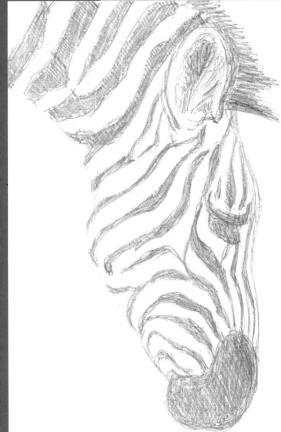

Zebra Cushion

DESIGN SIZE: 16in square
(40.6cm square)

STITCH COUNT:
white panel 43 x 228
black panel 70 x 228

MATERIALS

◆ white 14-count Zweigart canvas, 18in (46cm) square
◆ co-ordinating fabric for the back of the cushion
◆ size 20 tapestry needle
◆ rectangular or roller frame of a suitable size
◆ machine cotton for finishing
◆ cushion pad, 18in (46cm) square
◆ four large tassels

THREADS

Centre panel:
Anchor tapestry wool
8 skeins of 9800

Coats Aida crochet cotton
1 ball, colour 1

White panel:
Anchor soft embroidery cotton
2 skeins each of 01, 02

Anchor pearl cotton
1 skein of 01

(continued on page 56)

An area of zebra patterning in black and white is flanked by panels of bargello patterns, one using a variety of white or near-white threads, the other in tones of grey through to black. The zebra panel is drawn onto the canvas, and the side panels are worked from the charts. Large toning tassels finish the corners, and add a further touch of texture.

WORKING THE DESIGN

1 Enlarge the line drawing to 16 x 8in (40.6 x 20.3cm). The rows of stitches in the side panels must match up exactly with the zebra stripes; small adjustments may have to be made to the zebra pattern if there are any

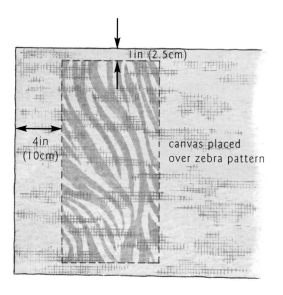

1in (2.5cm)

4in (10cm)

canvas placed over zebra pattern

Tracing the zebra pattern onto the canvas

Anchor Pearl cotton metallic
1 skein of 01

Anchor stranded cotton
1 skein of 01

Kreinik Metallics heavy braid
1 spool of 032

Black panel:
Anchor soft embroidery cotton
2 skeins of 403
1 skein each of: 400, 399, 234, 235, 236

Anchor Marlitt
2 skeins of 801

Kreinik blending filament
1 spool of 011HL

STRANDS USED

Tapestry wool (W in chart):
 1 thickness
Soft embroidery (SE): 1 thickness
Pearl cotton (PC): 2 strands
Stranded cotton (SC): 6 strands
Marlitt (M): 2 thicknesses
Kreinik blending filament (KBF):
 3 thicknesses
Kreinik heavy braid (KHB):
 1 thickness
Pearl cotton metallic (PCM):
 2 thicknesses
Crochet cotton (CC): 2 thicknesses

Where the chart gives more than one set of initials for any pattern (e.g. SE/M), the first row of the pattern should be worked in Soft Embroidery and the second row in Marlitt, and so on.

discrepancies. Place the canvas over the enlarged zebra pattern, leaving 4in (10cm) of canvas clear on the left-hand side, and 1in (2.5cm) at the top.

2 Make sure the rectangle formed by the pattern lines up with the weave of the canvas; then, using a grey waterproof pen, draw the design onto the canvas.

3 Attach the canvas to the frame (see page 12).

4 Work the black areas of the pattern first, using rows of straight stitches worked over six threads of the canvas. Then complete the remaining spaces using two strands of white crochet cotton, and the same size stitch.

5 Using the charts, complete the white panel to the left and the black and grey panel to the right. Refer to the code letters for the different threads (listed at left under 'Strands used'), and the keys for the colours.

6 Check your work for mistakes and loose ends, then remove the embroidery from the frame. Block the finished piece (see pages 15–16).

7 Cut an 18in (46cm) square of co-ordinating fabric.

8 With right sides facing, place the embroidery and the backing fabric together. Pin and tack carefully.

9 Machine-stitch as close to the embroidery as possible, leaving a good-sized opening in one side.

10 Trim all seams to ½in (1.25cm). Mitre the corners.

11 Turn the cushion right side out. Insert the pad and stitch up the opening using ladder stitch (see pages 106–7).

12 Attach a tassel to each corner; to make your own, see page 18.

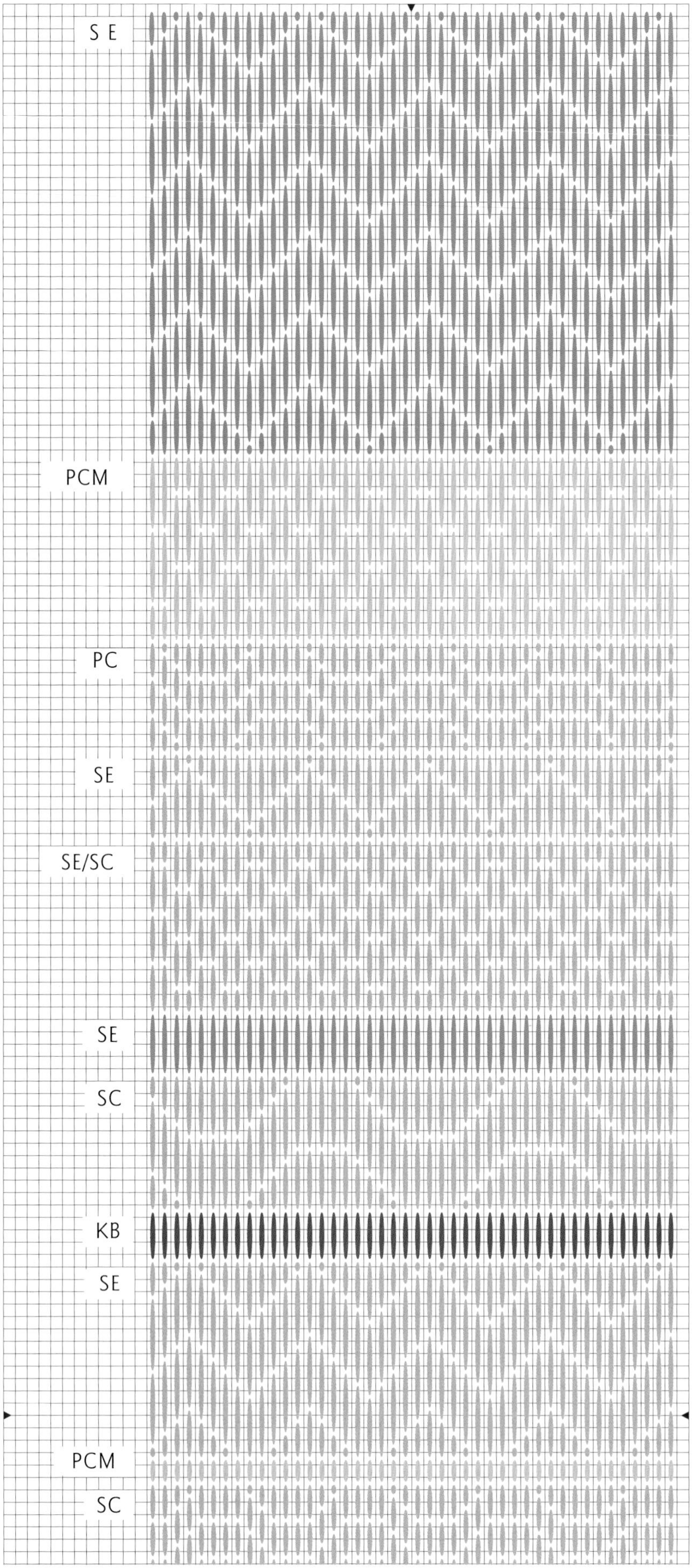

S E

PCM

PC

SE

SE/SC

SE

SC

KB

SE

PCM

SC

CHART A (TOP)

Join chart here

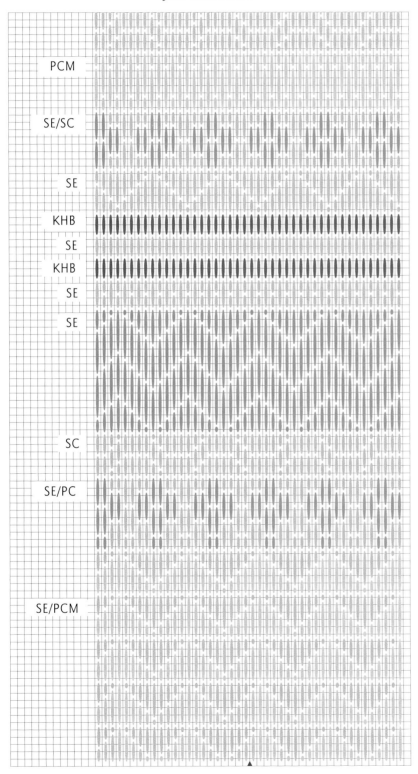

PCM

SE/SC

SE

KHB

SE

KHB

SE

SE

SC

SE/PC

SE/PCM

Zebra Cushion

(Left-hand panel)

01

01 Metallic

02

Kreinik 032

CHART A (BOTTOM)

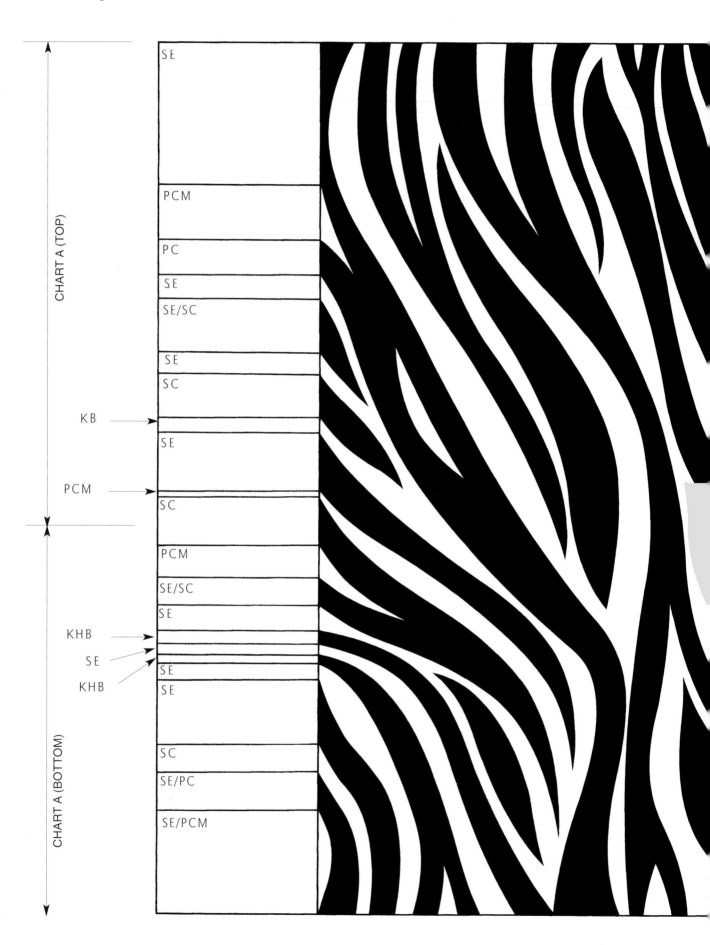

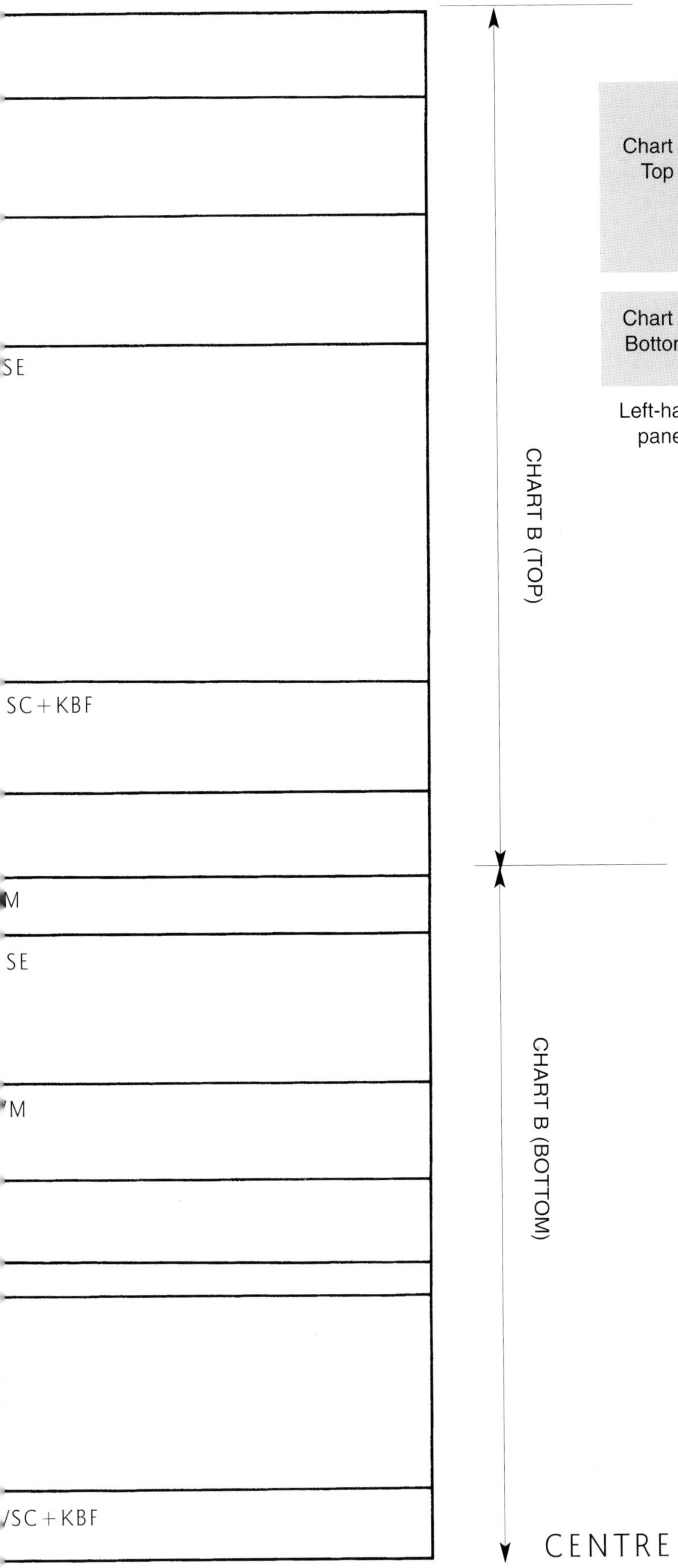

SE

SC+KBF

M

SE

'M

/SC+KBF

CHART B (TOP)

CHART B (BOTTOM)

Chart A
Top

Centre panel

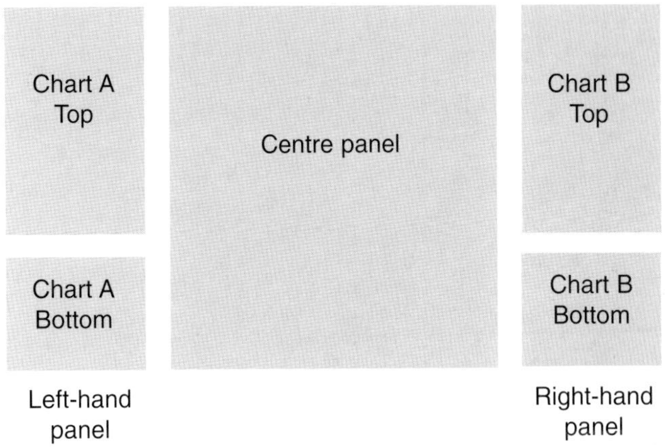

Chart B
Top

Chart A
Bottom

Chart B
Bottom

Left-hand
panel

Right-hand
panel

Follow the guide above (not drawn to scale)

for positioning of panels

CENTRE PANEL

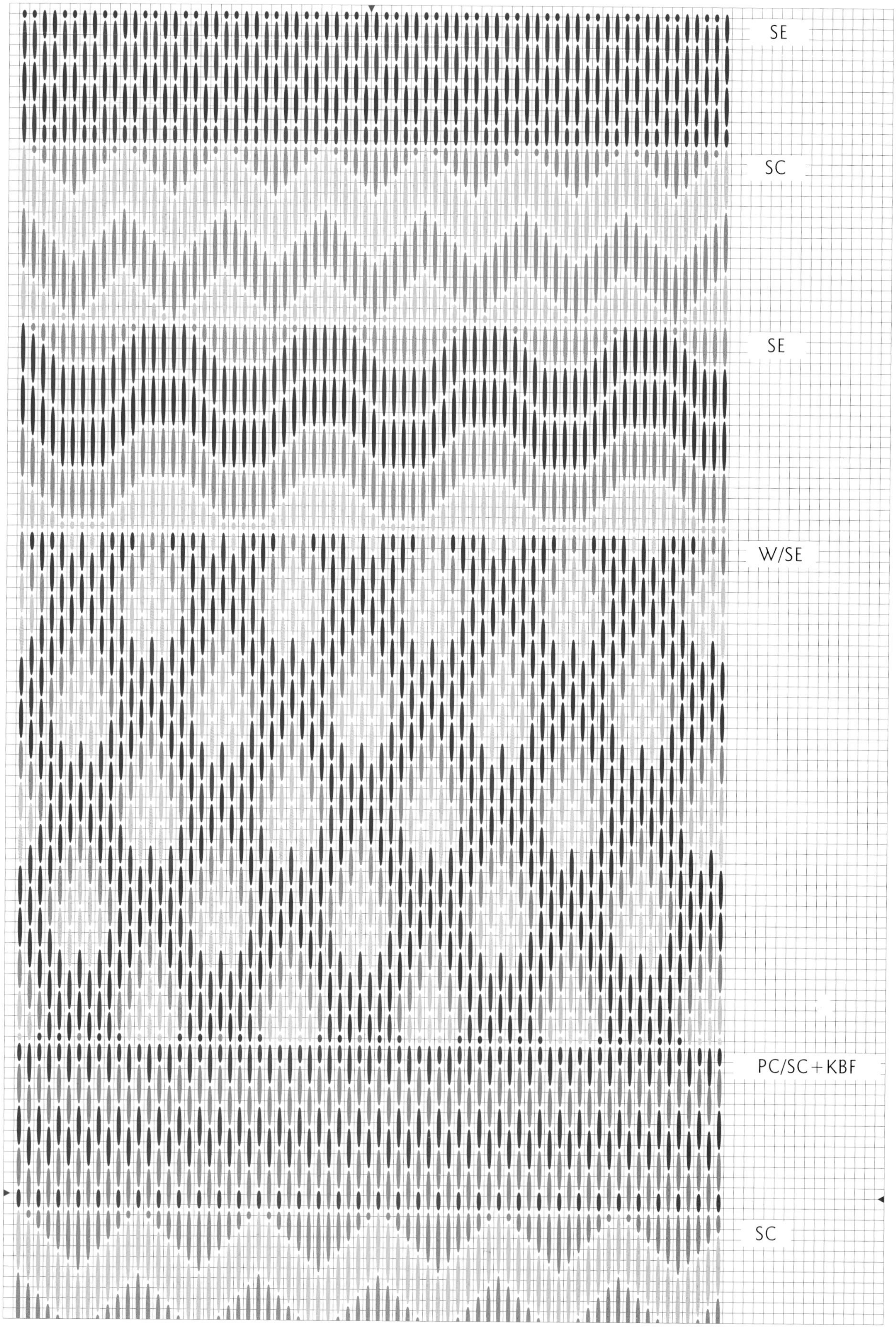

SE

SC

SE

W/SE

PC/SC+KBF

SC

CHART B (TOP)

Join chart here

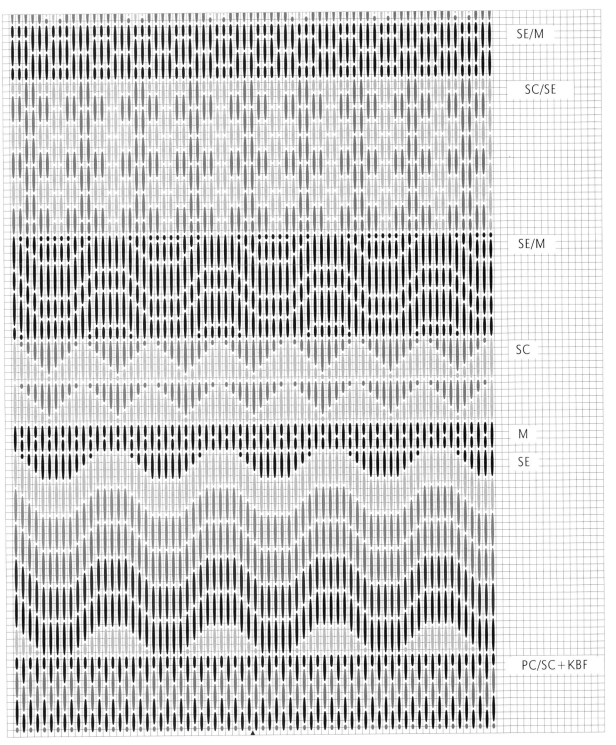

SE/M

SC/SE

SE/M

SC

M

SE

PC/SC+KBF

CHART B (BOTTOM)

Zebra Cushion

(Right-hand panel)

399	403	235
400	236	234

Fish and Water Panel

SKILL LEVEL 3

DESIGN SIZE: 11 x 15¼in
                (28 x 38.7cm)
STITCH COUNT: 160 x 216

MATERIALS

◆ white 14-count Zweigart canvas,
   17 x 21in (43.2 x 53.3cm)
◆ size 22 tapestry needle
◆ beading needle
◆ rectangular or roller frame of a
   suitable size

THREADS

DMC stranded cotton
3 skeins each of: 3750, 3756, 3766,
   3809, 3811
2 skeins each of: 720, 722, 807,
   3768, 3810
1 skein of 3808

Anchor space-dyed stranded cotton
2 skeins of 1212

Coats Diadem metallic braid
1 spool of 301 Silver

Coats Ophir metallic thread
1 spool of 301 Silver

Offray 3mm doubleface satin ribbon
2 yards/metres of 305 pale blue
2 yards/metres of 317 light turquoise

(continued on page 68)

Based on a Japanese woodcut, this panel with its swirling waves and colourful fish shows the development from a bargello pattern worked in one colour to a multicoloured treatment. Silver threads, satin ribbon and beads give the panel added richness. The design is drawn onto the canvas, rather than being charted.

WORKING THE DESIGN

1 Enlarge the line drawing to the suggested size. Place the canvas centrally over the enlarged drawing and, using a grey waterproof pen, transfer the design onto the canvas.

2 Attach your canvas to the frame (see page 12).

3 Using the coding shown for each area, begin stitching from the bottom of the panel. This will give you practice in fitting stitches to an irregular shape, using just one colour.

4 Check the coding carefully: letters denote patterns (according to the chart on page 68), numbers denote colours. There is one exception to this: **DSB**, where **D** denotes the stitch and **SB** denotes silver braid.

5 As you work the bargello patterns and the long-stitch areas, you might find it helpful to stroke the stitches from top to bottom with the end of a

MACHINE THREADS

To match both ribbons

DMC BEADS

I box each of:
VI 10 Blanc Pearl white
VI 07 317 Light silver
V3 04 939 Petrol blue

STRANDS USED

Stranded cotton: 6 strands
Space-dyed stranded cotton:
6 strands
Diadem: I thickness
Ophir: I thickness

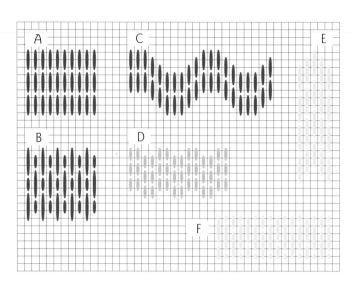

Key to drawing on pages 70–1

thumb or fingernail to spread the threads. If a twist occurs in the stitch, loosen it with your needle, carefully untwist the threads, and lay the thread in place again.

6 When the central panel is completed, cut two 15in (38cm) lengths of turquoise ribbon, and two 21in (54cm) lengths of the same colour.

7 Couch these in place centrally, as near as possible to the worked area, overlapping the ribbon at the corners. Leave the surplus ribbon ends free.

8 Work stitch F along the top and bottom as near to the ribbon as possible, and then work stitch E down each side. Both of these stitches are worked in Anchor 1212.

9 Cut two 15in (38cm) lengths of pale blue ribbon, and two 21in (54cm) lengths of the same colour.

10 Stitch in place as before, overlapping the previous turquoise ribbon, and placing as close to the stitched border as possible.

11 Fill the small empty square formed in each corner with **DSB** (see step 4).

12 Pull the remaining ribbon through to the back of the work and stitch in place securely on the back of the work. Trim any surplus ribbon.

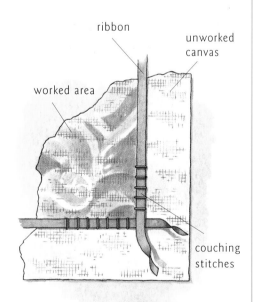

Couching the ribbon border

13 Work two rows of half cross-stitch or tent stitch along each side to finish the edge, using 3809.

14 Using a matching thread, stitch the silver and pearl beads in position, as shown in the photograph, to represent the spray from the waves.

15 Use pairs of petrol-blue beads for the centres of the eyes of the fish (see photograph).

16 Check for mistakes and loose ends, then remove your embroidery from the frame.

17 You may wish to stretch and mount your work (see pages 16–17). Alternatively, if you are not comfortable with this task, ask a professional framer to stretch, mount and frame it under glass for you.

Fish and Water Panel

pages 70–1

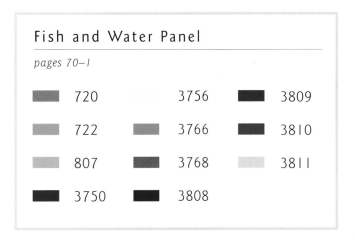

▰ 720	▰ 3756	▰ 3809
▰ 722	▰ 3766	▰ 3810
▰ 807	▰ 3768	▰ 3811
▰ 3750	▰ 3808	

TOP

BOTTOM

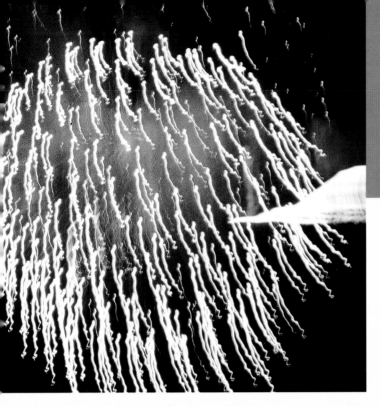

Florentine Pincushion

DESIGN SIZE: 5¾in square
                (14.6cm square)
STITCH COUNT: 104 x 102

MATERIALS

- white 18-count Zweigart canvas, 9in (23cm) square
- co-ordinating fabric for the back
- size 22 tapestry needle
- beading needle
- rectangular or roller frame of a suitable size
- machine cotton for finishing
- microfibre stuffing

THREADS

DMC stranded cotton
1 skein each of: 758, 356, 503, 500, 436, 738

DMC perlé size 5
1 skein each of: 754, 355, 502, 504

MILL HILL BEADS

Antique glass beads
1 box of 03003 Cranberry

Glass pebble beads
1 box of 05270 Bottle green

STRANDS USED:

Stranded cotton: 6 strands
Perlé: 1 thickness

A sheet of hand-made marbled paper, sourced from a small manufacturer in Florence, was the starting point for this oversized pincushion. The subtle shades of the paper and its irregular pattern, reminiscent of Bargello patterns, inspired a design that can be translated in several ways. Try using the panel as the top of a box, or make a smaller pincushion from just half of it; alternatively, use the area of pattern to cover a small notebook. The pincushion is finished with small beaded tassels at each corner.

WORKING THE DESIGN

1 Attach your canvas to the frame (see page 12).

2 Find the centre of your canvas by measuring in both directions, and mark lightly with a pencil.

3 Find the centre of the chart by using the centre marks, and mark with a pencil.

4 Starting from the centre, work the double row of cross stitch which

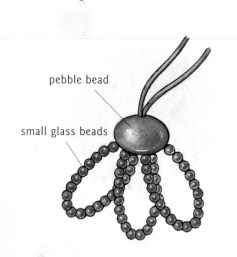

pebble bead

small glass beads

Detail of beaded tassel

divides the two panels. Count the crosses carefully, and continue with the line of crosses around the pattern areas.

5 Follow the chart and fill in the areas of pattern, starting at either the top or the bottom to ensure that the position of the pattern is correct.

6 When both panels are completed, check for mistakes and loose ends, and remove your embroidery from the frame. It should not be necessary to block such a small piece of work.

7 Trim the surplus canvas to ½in (1.25cm), and cut a piece of backing fabric to match this in size.

8 With the right sides facing, tack and then machine-stitch the two pieces together. Make sure that your stitching is as close to the embroidery as possible, and stop precisely at each corner. Leave part of one side open.

9 Mitre the corners, and turn the pincushion to the right side.

10 Fill firmly with stuffing, pushing it well into the corners. Stitch up the opening using ladder stitch (see pages 106–7).

11 To make the beaded tassels, thread 20 small beads onto a matching thread, and tie to make a loop, but do not cut the thread. Thread a further twenty beads onto the thread and tie off as before. Repeat once more.
Take the two ends of thread through a pebble bead before attaching to the pincushion.

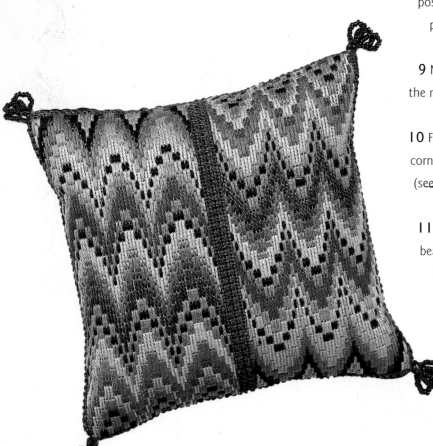

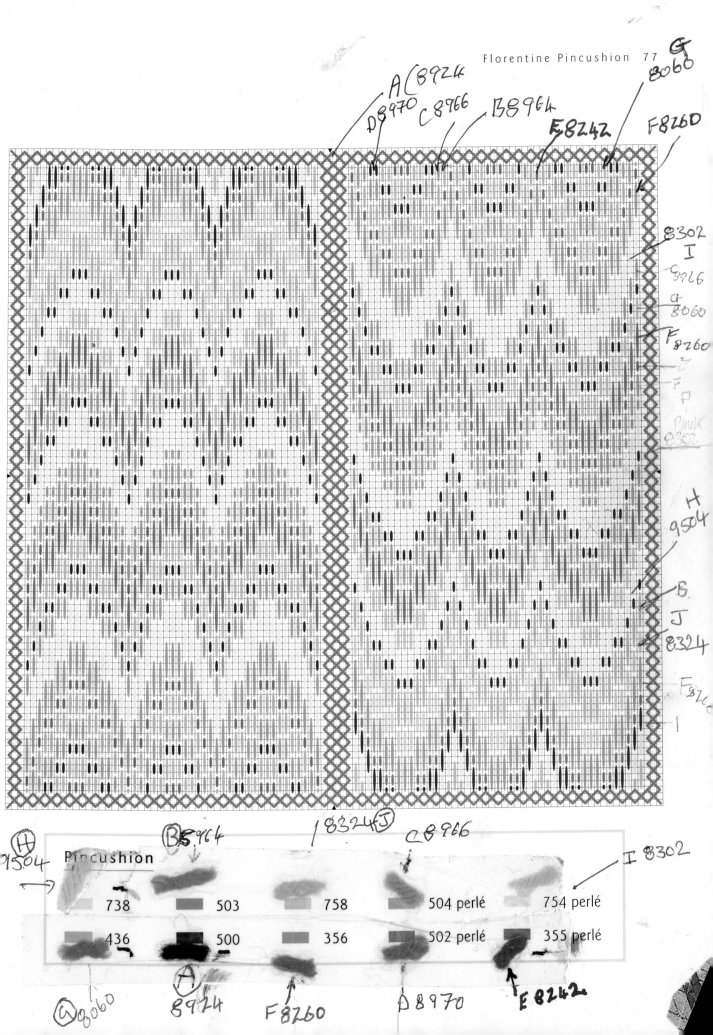

G 8060

A C8924
D8970 C 8966   B 8964
E 8242   F 8260

8302
I
8966
a
8060
F 8260

H
9504

B
J
8324

F 8260

H
9504

8324 J   C 8966

B 8964

I 8302

Pincushion

| | 738 | | 503 | | 758 | | 504 perlé | | 754 perlé |
| | 436 | | 500 | | 356 | | 502 perlé | | 355 perlé |

G 8060   A 8924   F 8260   D 8970   E 8242

Two Topiary Panels

DESIGN SIZE: 4⅞ x 9⅜in
                 (12.4 x 23.6cm)
STITCH COUNT: 88 x 168

MATERIALS

◆ white Zweigart 18-count canvas:
  2 pieces 9 x 13in (23 x 33cm)
◆ size 22 tapestry needle
◆ rectangular or roller frame of a
  suitable size

THREADS

Anchor stranded cotton
Spherical tree
  2 skeins each of: 246, 875
  1 skein each of: 1031, 9159,
  1038, 920, 258, 161, 1034, 1036,
  1050, 213, 214, 216
Conical tree
as above, plus 1 skein each of:
  254, 256

KREINIK METALLICS

Medium Braid, size 16
1 spool of 002 Gold for each design

MILL HILL GLASS SEED BEADS

1 box of 00557 Gold

STRANDS USED

Stranded cotton: 6 strands
Gold braid: 1 thickness

The geometrical shapes of topiary, and the many different shades of green which are found in it, were the starting point for these two formal panels. The addition of gold thread and beads gives a rich, icon-like effect to the designs.

WORKING THE DESIGN

1 Attach your canvas to the frame (see page 12).

2 Find the centre of the canvas by measuring in both directions, and mark with a pencil.

3 Find the middle of the chart by using the centre marks, and mark with a pencil.

4 Begin stitching from the middle, stitching the tree first, and leaving the beads until all the stitching is completed.

5 When the tree, trunk and pot are completed, work the background patterns, finishing with the border.

6 Add the beads, stitching them at regular intervals, as shown on the chart.

7 Check for mistakes and loose ends and remove your embroidery from the frame. Block the finished pieces.

8 You may wish to stretch and frame the work, following the directions given on pages 16–17. If this seems too daunting, ask a professional framer to stretch, mount and frame the panels for you. It is advisable to stipulate that they are mounted under glass to protect them from dust.

Spherical tree

	1031
	9159
	1038
	920
	258
	161
	1034
	1036
	246
	Gold
	1050
	213
	875
	214
	216
⊙ ⊙	Mill Hill beads

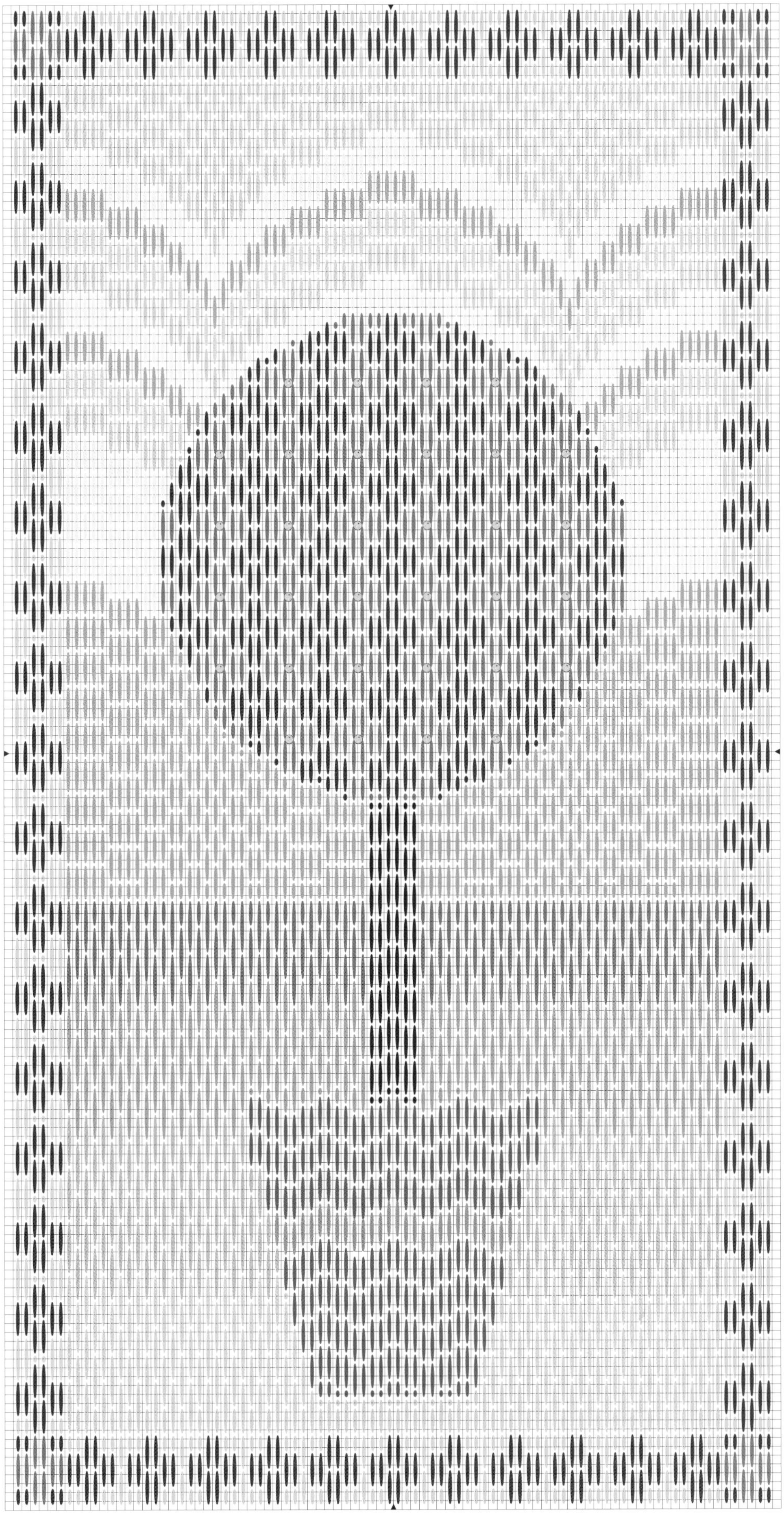

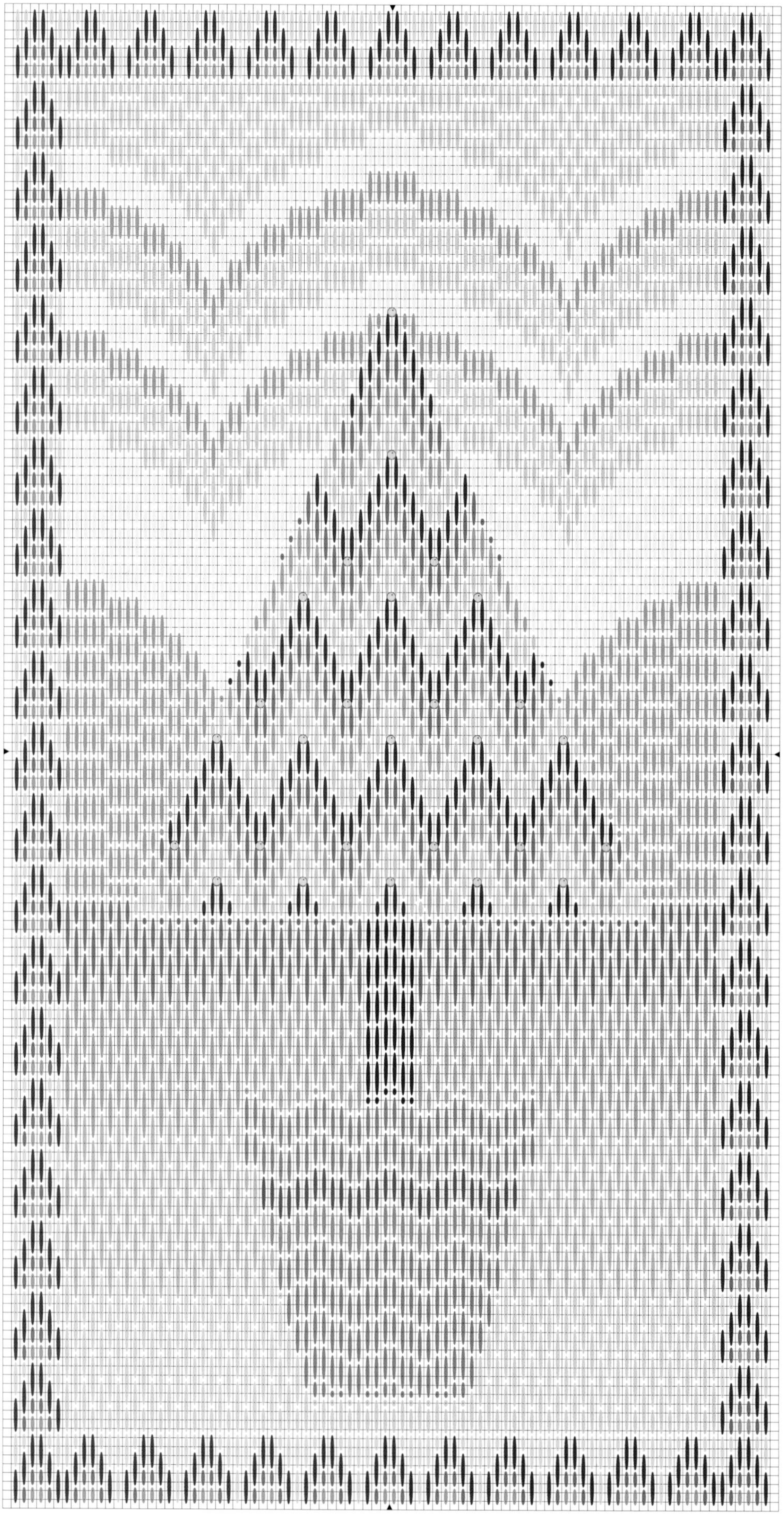

Conical tree

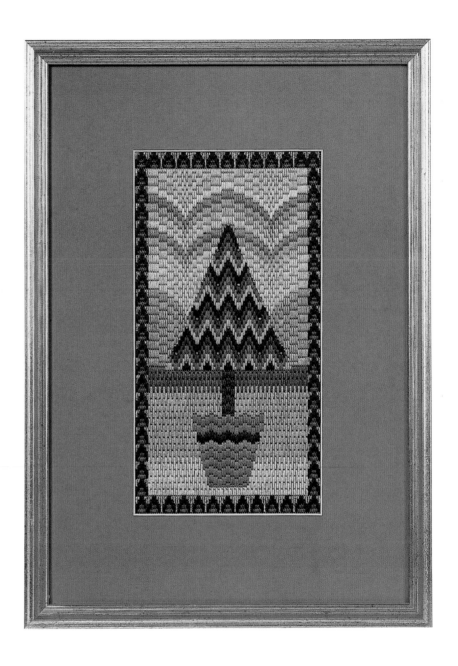

1031

9159

1038

920

258

161

1034

1036

246

Gold

1050

213

875

214

216

254

256

Mill Hill beads

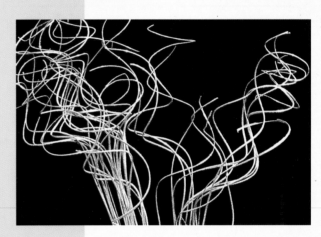

Curtain Tie-Back

A ribbon-wrapped branch, worked in two colours of marble at the entrance to Siena Cathedral, was the starting point. The simple bargello pattern used throughout makes this an easy project. You could try working the background in several shades of a suitable colour, instead of the white. Use the same design for a matching bell-pull; three repeats of the central motif might make an interesting cushion panel.

SKILL LEVEL 1

DESIGN SIZE: 4¼ x 21¼in
                (10.8 x 54cm)
STITCH COUNT: 60 x 298

MATERIALS

◆ white 14-count Zweigart canvas,
  6½ x 25in (16.5 x 63.5cm)
◆ Pelform stiffening,
  4¼ x 21¼in (10.8 x 54cm)
◆ co-ordinating fabric for lining
◆ size 20 tapestry needle
◆ roller frame of a suitable size
◆ machine cotton for finishing
◆ two small brass rings

THREADS

Anchor tapestry wool
3 skeins of 8902
1 skein each of: 8914, 8918,
  8808, 8904

Coats Aida crochet cotton
1 ball of colour 1 White

STRANDS USED

Tapestry wool: 1 thickness
Aida crochet cotton: 2 strands

WORKING THE DESIGN

1 Attach the narrow ends of the canvas to the frame (see page 12).

2 Find the centre of the canvas strip by measuring, and mark the middle of the narrow end with a pencil.

3 Starting with the outer edge of the design, and chart 1, begin stitching 2in (5cm) away from the short end of the canvas.

4 Follow this with the outlines of the ribbons and branches, counting the unworked canvas threads carefully and making sure that this section of the design is centralized within the worked outer edge.

5 Fill in the ribbons and branches using the appropriate stitches and colours. Do not stitch the background yet.

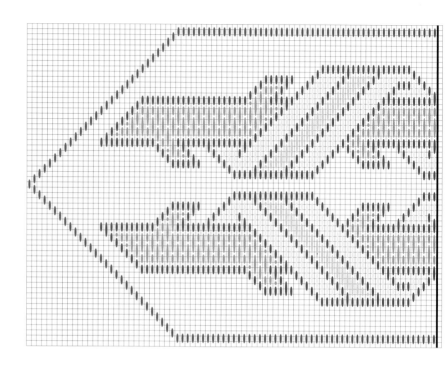

Chart 1

6 Move to chart 2 and repeat this area of the design four times. Work as before, matching the outlines carefully.

7 Finally work the area of the design on chart 3. You will have worked the outer line along with the central area, and should now be ready to complete the background.

8 This is worked in two strands of crochet cotton as shown in the detail chart below left, and particular care must be taken to keep the thread free of twists. Using the same stitch as the branches and starting in the centre of the design, fill in the background, fitting the stitch to the worked shapes.

9 The area stitched gives an average-sized tie-back, but you could change the length by working fewer or more repeats from chart 2.

10 Check for mistakes and loose ends, then remove your embroidery from the frame. Block the finished piece (see pages 15–16).

11 Cut the Pelform stiffening to fit the outer edge of the stitched areas exactly, mitring the ends to match the tie-back.

Detail chart

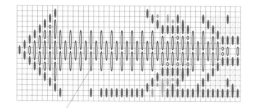

background filling stitch

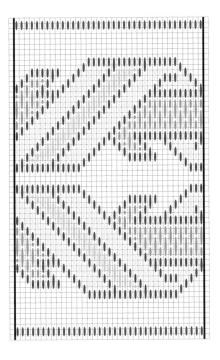

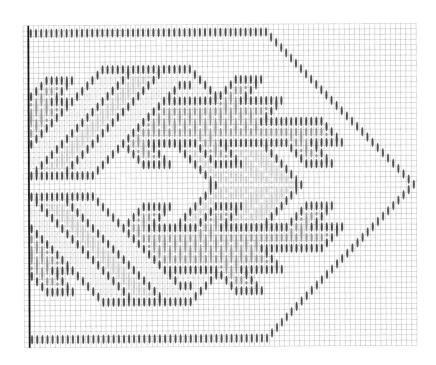

Chart 2; repeat 4 times — *Chart 3*

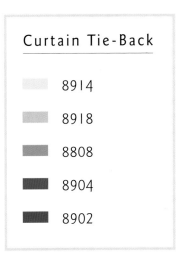

Curtain Tie-Back

8914

8918

8808

8904

8902

12 Lay the embroidery face down on a clean surface and, ensuring that it is centred, place the Pelform stiffening on top. Peel off a small section of the backing paper, position the point and align the strip with the edge of the worked area.

13 Continue to peel off the backing and position the Pelform a little at a time until you reach the other end. Press into place. Trim the surplus canvas ½in (1.25cm) away from the worked edge.

14 Remove the remaining backing from the top side of the Pelform and turn the surplus canvas onto the adhesive surface, mitring the corners where it is necessary.

15 Cut a strip of lining fabric ½in (1.25cm) larger all round than the stiffened embroidery. Place the lining fabric strip face down and centre the stiffened tie-back on top of it. Press into place. Turn under the surplus fabric to make a small hem, and slip-stitch the two pieces of fabric together.

16 Sew a small brass ring onto each end of the reverse side of the tie-back so that you can hang it neatly around your curtain.

Vibrant Pink Cushion

SKILL LEVEL 2

DESIGN SIZE: 10¾in square
                (27.3cm square)

STITCH COUNT: 154 x 154

MATERIALS

◆ white 14-count Zweigart canvas,
  15in (38cm) square
◆ co-ordinating fabric for borders
  and back: one 16in (40.6cm) square,
  and four strips measuring 3 x 16in
  (7.6 x 40.6cm)
◆ size 20 tapestry needle
◆ rectangular frame or roller frame of
  suitable size
◆ machine cotton for finishing
◆ cushion pad, 16in (40.6cm) square

THREADS

Anchor tapestry wool
3 skeins each of: 8552, 8550, 8488

Anchor perlé size 5
2 skeins of 870

Caron Watercolours
1 skein each of: 158 Grape,
084 African Sunset

STRANDS USED

Tapestry wool: 1 thickness
Perlé: 2 thicknesses
Watercolours: Grape 2 strands,
African Sunset 3 strands

A combination of patterns from African woven boxes and vibrant colour from a decorative cabbage were the inspiration for this exciting cushion. The worked area on its own would make a small cushion, or it could be extended, as in the photograph, by adding a fabric border to make a larger one.

WORKING THE DESIGN

1 Attach your canvas square to the frame (see page 12).

2 Find the centre of the canvas by measuring in both directions, and mark the centre with a pencil, lightly.

3 Find the middle of the chart by using the centre marks, and mark with a pencil.

4 Begin stitching from the middle, paying attention to the direction of the stitches. You might find it less confusing to work the vertical diamonds first, followed by the horizontal ones, and then finally fill the centres.

5 Complete the central area before working the border. Take particular care with the bands of pattern, as the stitches change in length throughout.

6 Check for mistakes and loose ends, then remove your embroidery from the frame. Block the finished piece (see pages 15–16).

7 Trim the surplus canvas to ½in (1.25cm).

8 Cut four 4 strips of co-ordinating fabric, 3 x 16in (7.6 x 40.6cm), and one 16in (40.6cm) square.

9 With the right sides facing, tack one strip in place centrally along each edge of the square. Leave the ends free. Stitch as close to the embroidery as possible using a matching machine thread, stopping precisely at each corner.

10 Press the seams away from the embroidery.

11 With right sides of strips together, mitre the corners. Trim the surplus fabric ½in (1.25cm) from the stitching and press the seams open.

12 Place the front and the back of the cushion together with the right sides facing. Pin and tack ½in (1.25cm) from the edges. Machine-stitch, leaving a good-sized opening in one side.

13 Mitre the corners. Turn the cushion right side out. Insert the pad and stitch up the opening using ladder stitch (see pages 106–7).

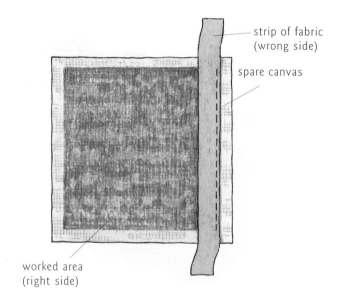

strip of fabric
(wrong side)

spare canvas

worked area
(right side)

Tacking on the first border strip

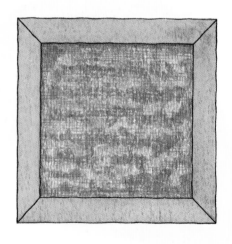

*The completed mitred border, seen
from the right side*

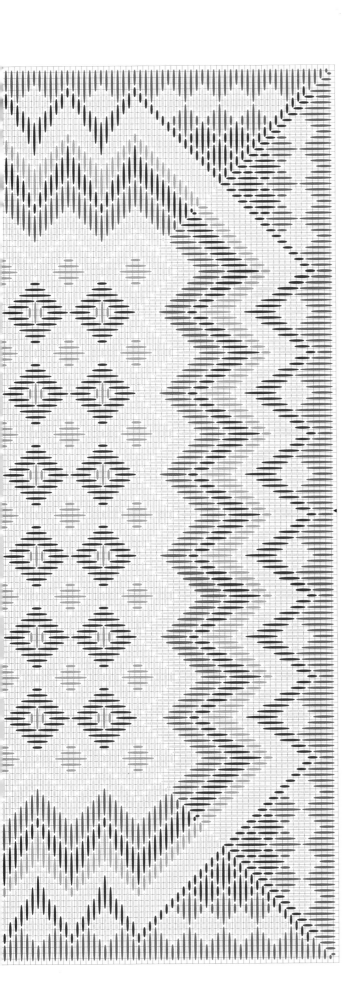

Vibrant Pink Cushion

▬	8552
▬	8550
▬	8488
▬	Anchor perlé 870
▬	158 Grape
▬	084 African Sunset

Diamond Box Lid

DESIGN SIZE: 8¼ x 3⁵⁄₁₆in
                 (21 x 8.4cm)
STITCH COUNT: 149 x 60

MATERIALS

- white 18-count Zweigart canvas, 7 x 12in (17.8 x 30.5cm)
- size 24 tapestry needle
- rectangular frame or roller frame of suitable size
- Framecraft WHB1 hobby box with drop-on lid

THREADS

Caron Watercolours
1 hank of 006 Amethyst

Coats Reflecta
1 spool of 5233

Anchor stranded cotton
1 skein each of: 1066, 123, 117, 1064, 112, 121, 1062, 100, 118, 1060, 98, 119, 109

STRANDS USED

Stranded cotton: 6 strands
Watercolours: 1 ply *(this is a 3-ply thread, so must be divided)*
Reflecta: 2 strands

This box top, with its precise squares which appear to float against the wave-patterned background, is based on a collection of very neatly woven boxes. They are of African origin, and suggest many more ideas for further projects. The diamond motif could be repeated several times to form a bell-pull, or it could provide an area of pattern on the end of a place mat.

WORKING THE DESIGN

1 Attach your canvas to the frame (see page 12).

2 Find the centre of the canvas by measuring in both directions, and mark the centre lightly with a pencil.

3 Find the middle of the chart by using the centre marks, and mark with a pencil.

4 Work the large diamond motifs, then the smaller wave pattern behind them. Starting from the central point of the large upper diamond, work the background pattern, followed by the small diamond at the bottom. Complete by working the border, using one strand of Watercolours.

5 Finally, finish by back-stitching, as shown by the black lines on the chart, with two strands of Reflecta.

6 Check for mistakes and loose ends, then remove your embroidery from the frame. Block the finished piece (see pages 15–16).

7 Mount your work following the instructions supplied with the box.

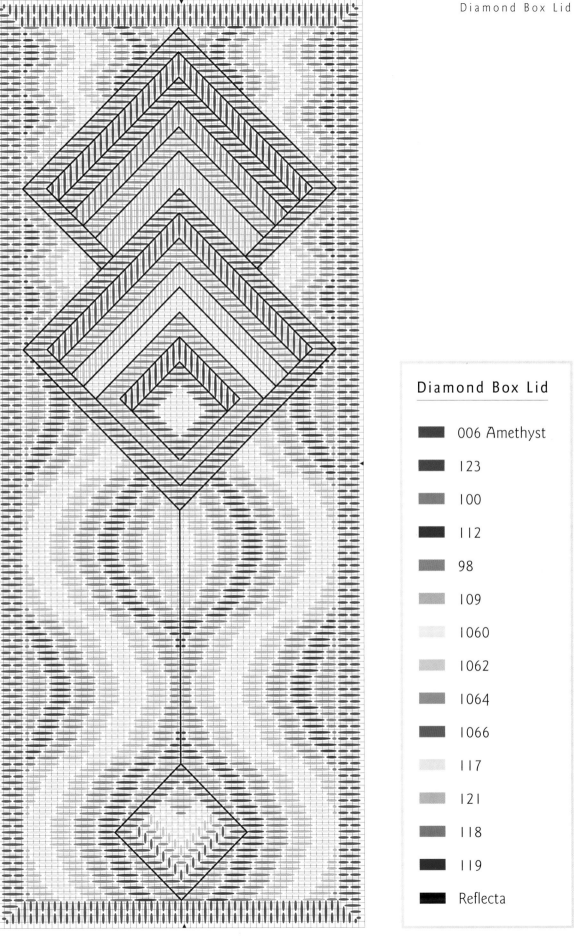

Diamond Box Lid

▰	006 Amethyst
▰	123
▰	100
▰	112
▰	98
▰	109
▰	1060
▰	1062
▰	1064
▰	1066
▰	117
▰	121
▰	118
▰	119
▰	Reflecta

Glossary of Stitches

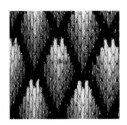

Although bargello embroidery is basically satin stitch (the length of the stitches being governed by the size of the canvas and by the pattern), one or two other stitches have been used in the projects in order to add interest. This section details the other stitches used, and concludes with a repertoire of bargello patterns which may help to inspire your own designs.

BACKSTITCH

This stitch has been used in some projects to outline and give definition to some of the shapes.

Following the diagram, first bring the needle up through the canvas a stitch-length along the line you wish to work. (I usually work this stitch over *two* canvas threads.) Take the needle back through the canvas at your designated starting point, drawing the thread through so that you now have a single complete stitch. Finally, bring the needle up again through the canvas a stitch-length ahead of the last. Your stitches should be neat and even in length to match the bargello stitches which you are outlining.

CROSS STITCH

This is usually completed in two stages. Stitch a row of diagonal stitches, working over the required number of threads of the canvas, until you reach the end; then return along the same row, stitching a reverse diagonal across the first. You can use this method horizontally or vertically, but always make sure that the top arms of the crosses point in the same direction.

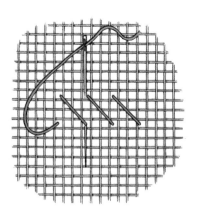

Cross stitch, step 1

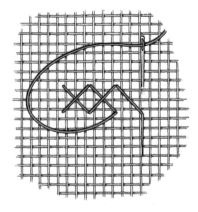

Cross stitch, step 2

Backstitch

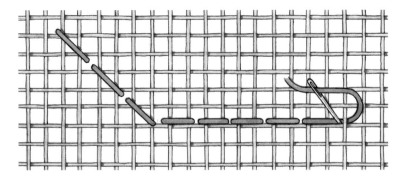

COUCHING

Couching is normally used to secure your thread to a piece of fabric, or for stitching an outline, but in this book it has been used to attach narrow satin ribbon to the canvas, thus forming an outline.

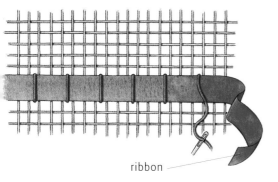

ribbon

Fig 1

The ribbon is couched by holding it down with a second, finer thread stitched at right angles over the ribbon, like tiny bridges, to hold it in place. To achieve the best result, make sure that these stitches are evenly spaced; it helps to count the threads of the canvas as you stitch.

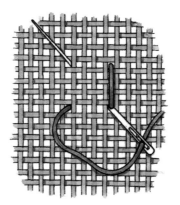

Fig 2

FOUR-SIDED STITCH

Each four-sided stitch is worked over a square composed of 4 x 4 threads of the facric, working from right to left.

Bring the needle up at the lower right-hand corner, insert the needle four threads up vertically, and bring it out four threads to the left of the starting point (Fig. 1).

Insert the needle at the bottom right-hand corner and bring up at the top left (Fig. 2).

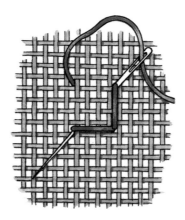

Fig 3

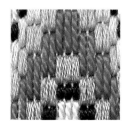

The remaining two sides of the square are worked in a similar way (Figs 3 and 4).

Repeat these stages to work a line of stitches (Fig 5).

When turning a corner, it is better to work in an anti-clockwise direction. A neater corner is produced by turning down rather than up (Fig 6).

SLIP STITCH

This simple stitch is used to finish hems or close openings, though for the latter I prefer to use ladder stitch (described next). Bring together the two edges of fabric or canvas which you wish to join, and stitch a line of small, diagonal stitches through both layers until the hem is completed or the opening closed.

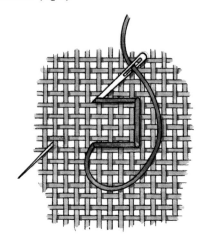

Fig 4

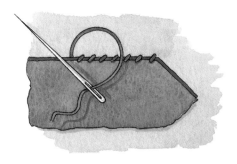

Slip stitch

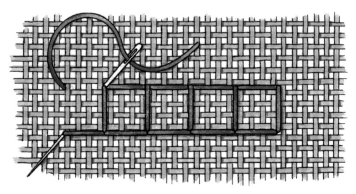

Fig 5

LADDER STITCH

This stitch is also used to close openings, but without showing a trace of the stitch itself on the resulting seam. Following the diagram, begin at one end of the opening. If you are working on fabric, take a small stitch along the edge of the near piece of fabric, then a second along the edge of the far piece of fabric, so that the second stitch begins opposite the end of the first. Work several stitches in this way, pulling up the thread as you work so that the stitches disappear.

Fig 6

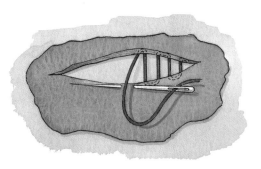

Ladder stitch

vertical threads of the canvas, with a gap of two threads between each group.

For the second row, fit the stitch over four threads into the two-thread gap between the groups in the previous row. Work compensation stitches at the top and bottom of an area to achieve a neat edge.

Alternate rows can be worked in contrasting colours if desired.

Continue until you have a closed seam, and fasten off securely.

HUNGARIAN STITCH

The stitches described above are used in the various projects in the book, either in the actual embroidery or as part of the finishing process, but the following stitch is the one which supposedly began the whole technique of bargello work. You will find it used in one of the projects.

Work this stitch in horizontal rows in groups of three stitches over two, four and two

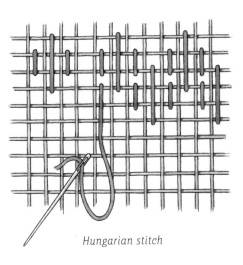

Hungarian stitch

Bargello Patterns

The following pages are devoted to a wide selection of bargello patterns – some of them derived from early examples – with which you can experiment. Try changing the number of threads over which each pattern is worked, or treating a pattern in either bright or subtle ranges of colour. Turn the pattern at right angles to itself, as I did in the Coasters and the Pink Cushion, but most of all be inventive, and play with colour, scale and texture to create something new.

The dots in these charts show where the repeat of the pattern begins and ends.

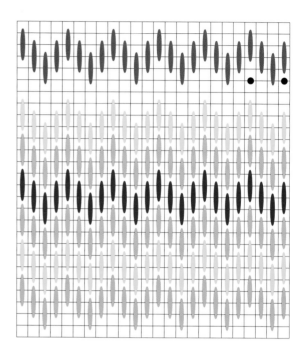

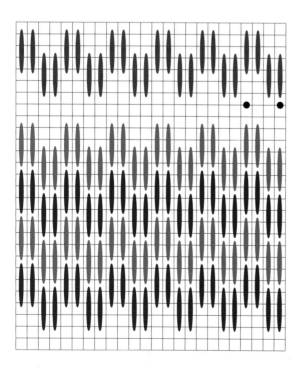

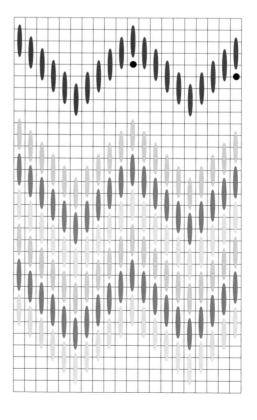

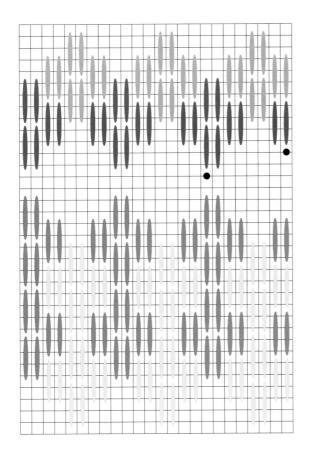

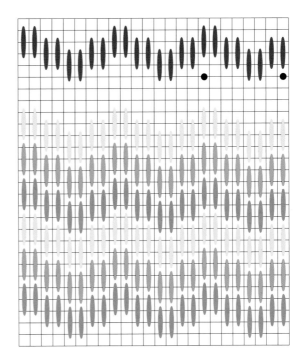

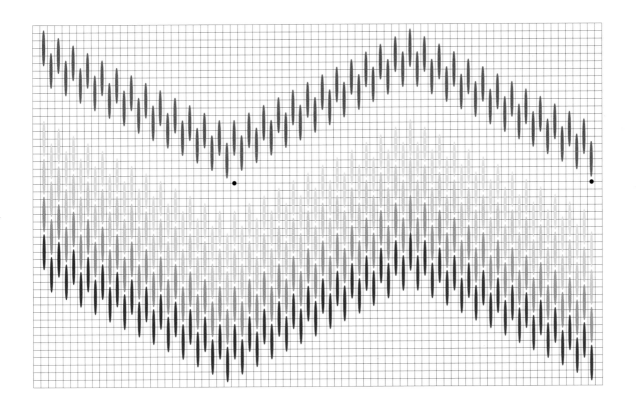

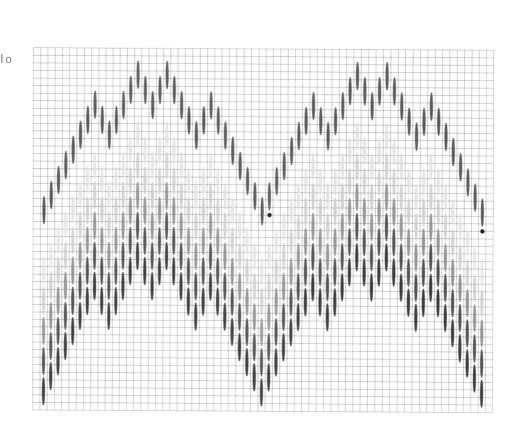

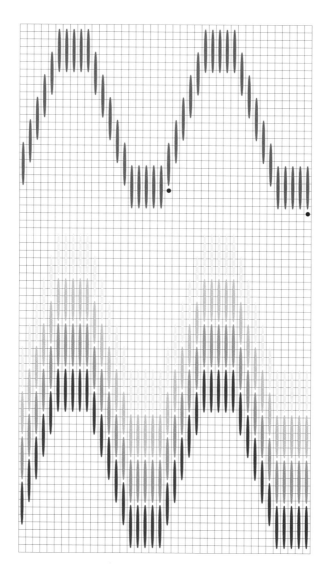

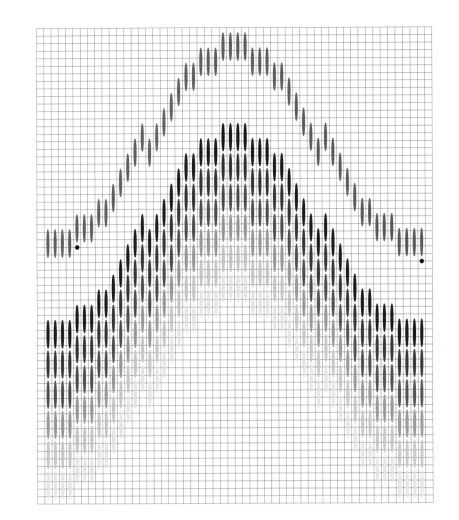

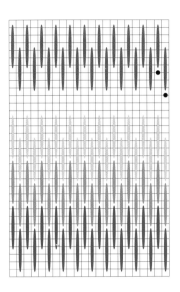

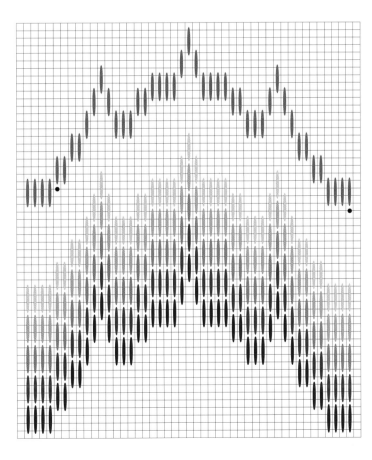

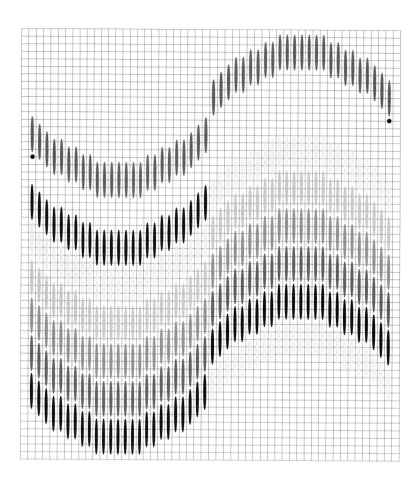

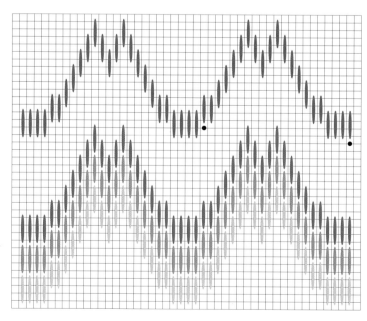

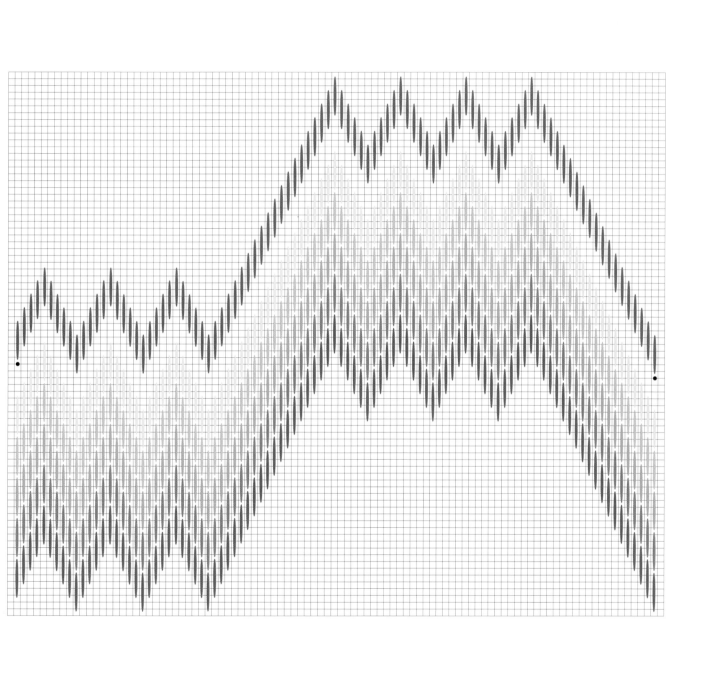

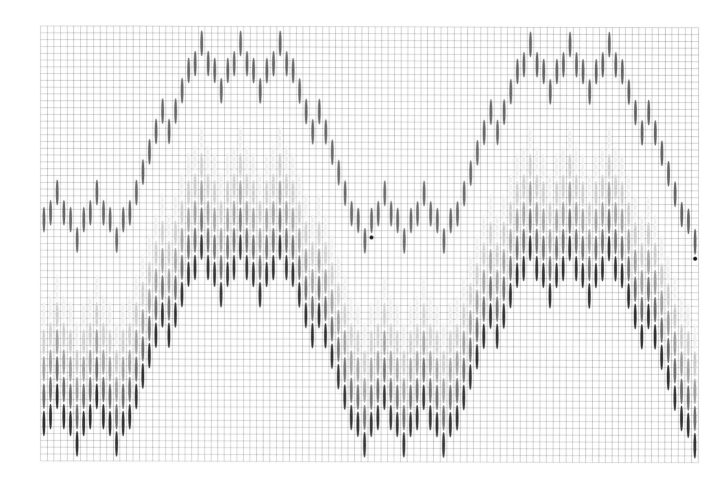

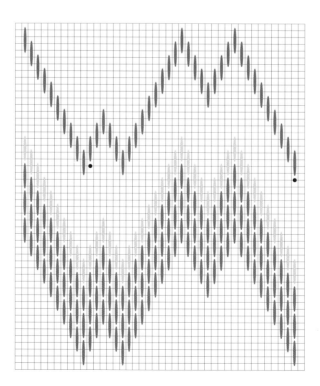

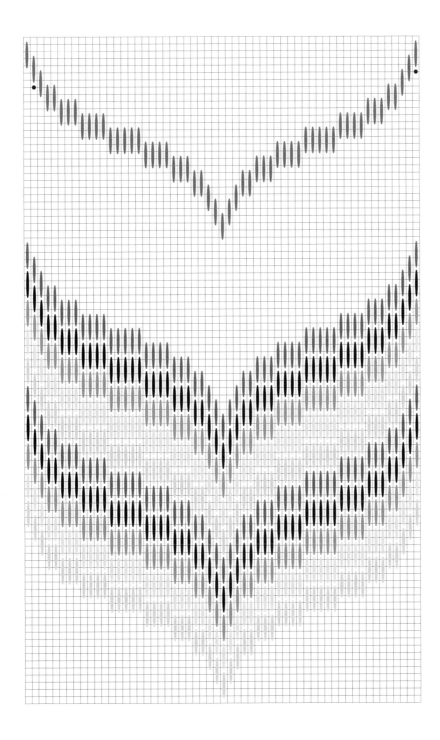

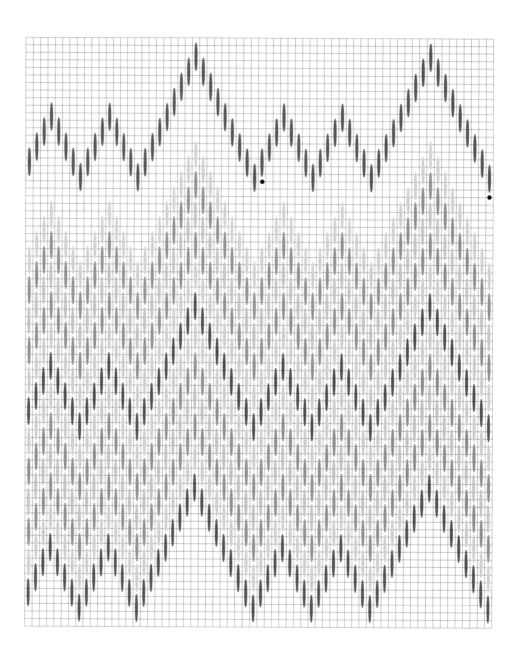

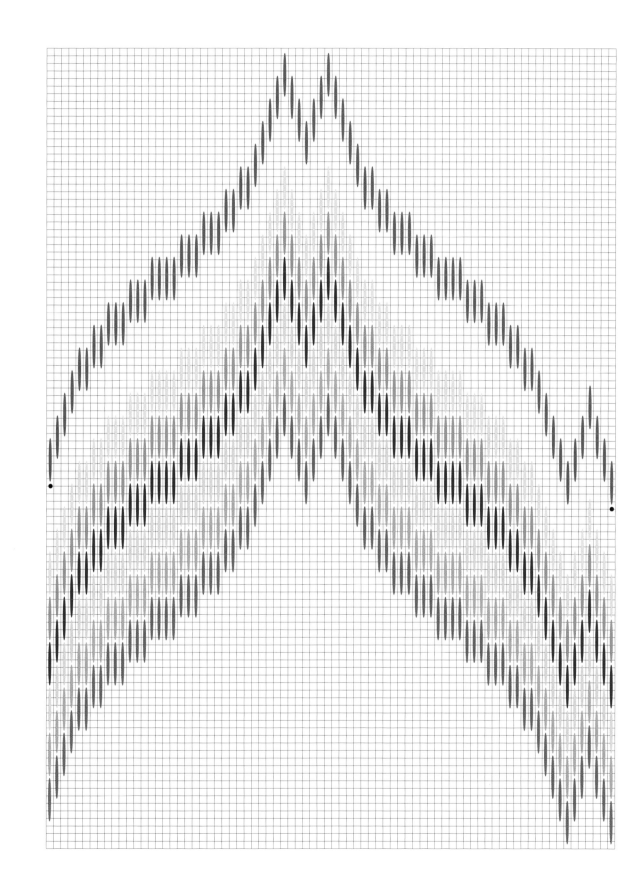

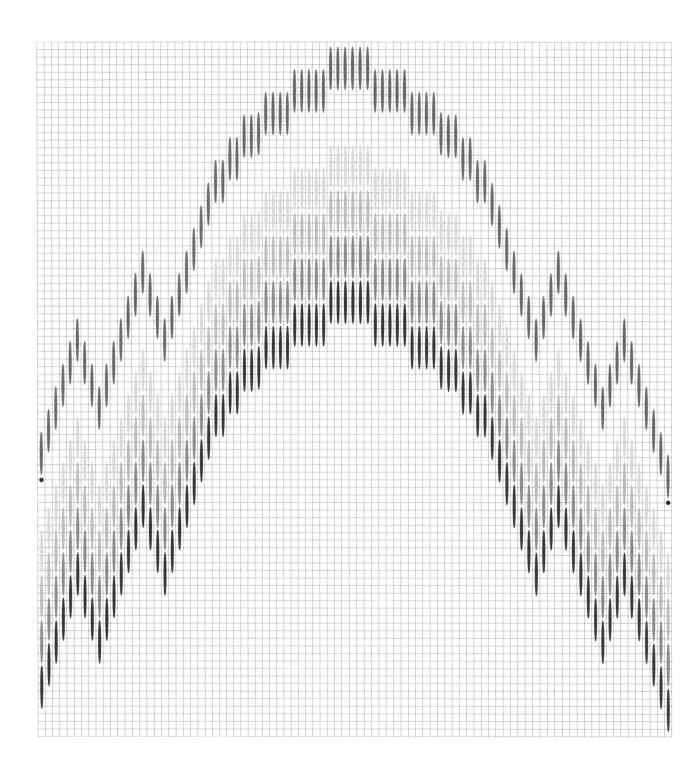

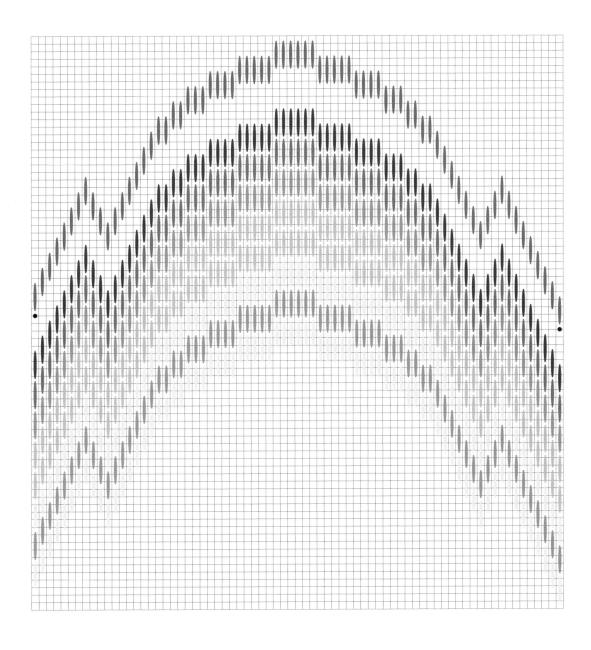

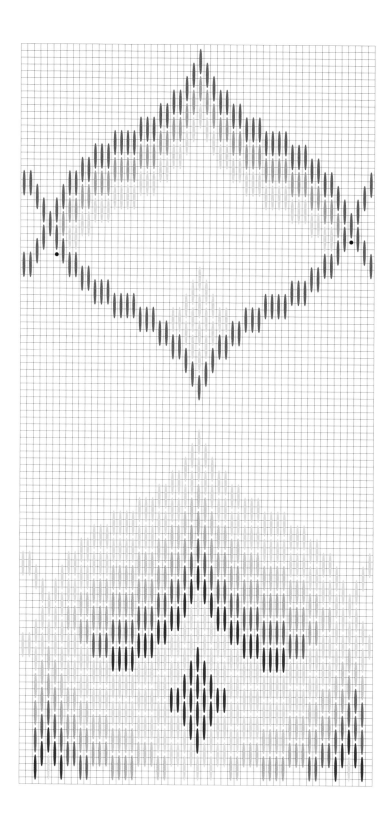

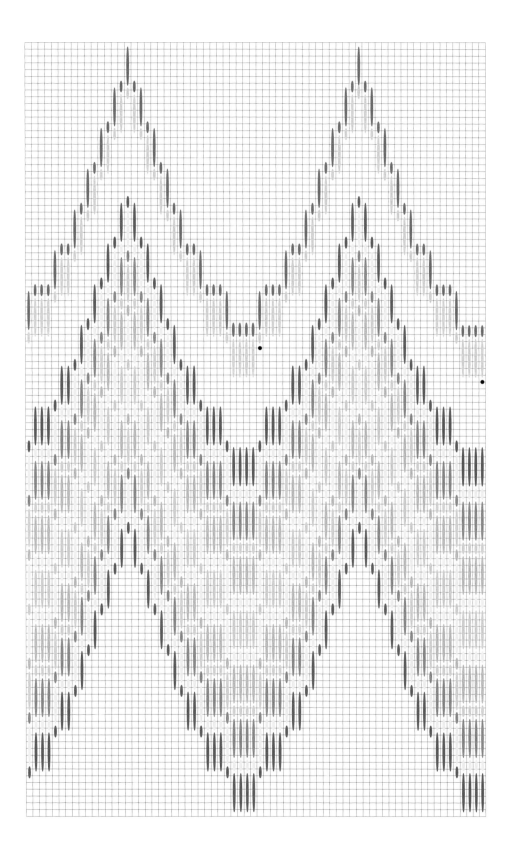

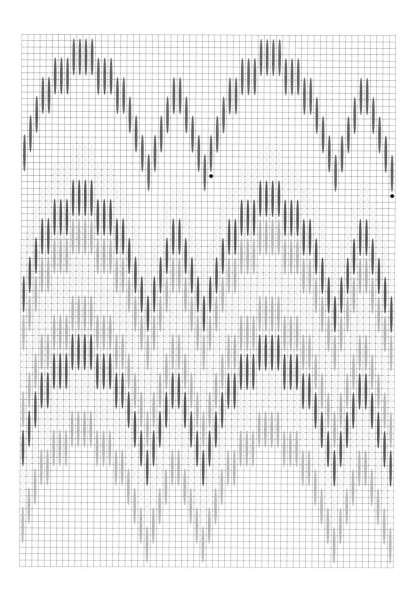

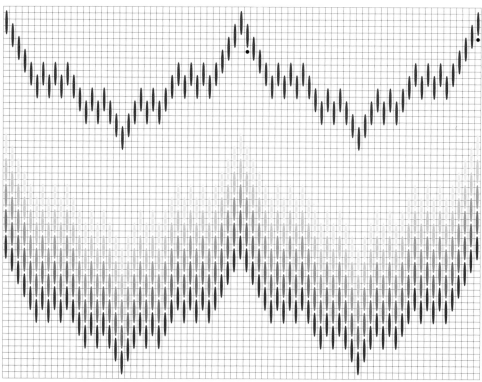

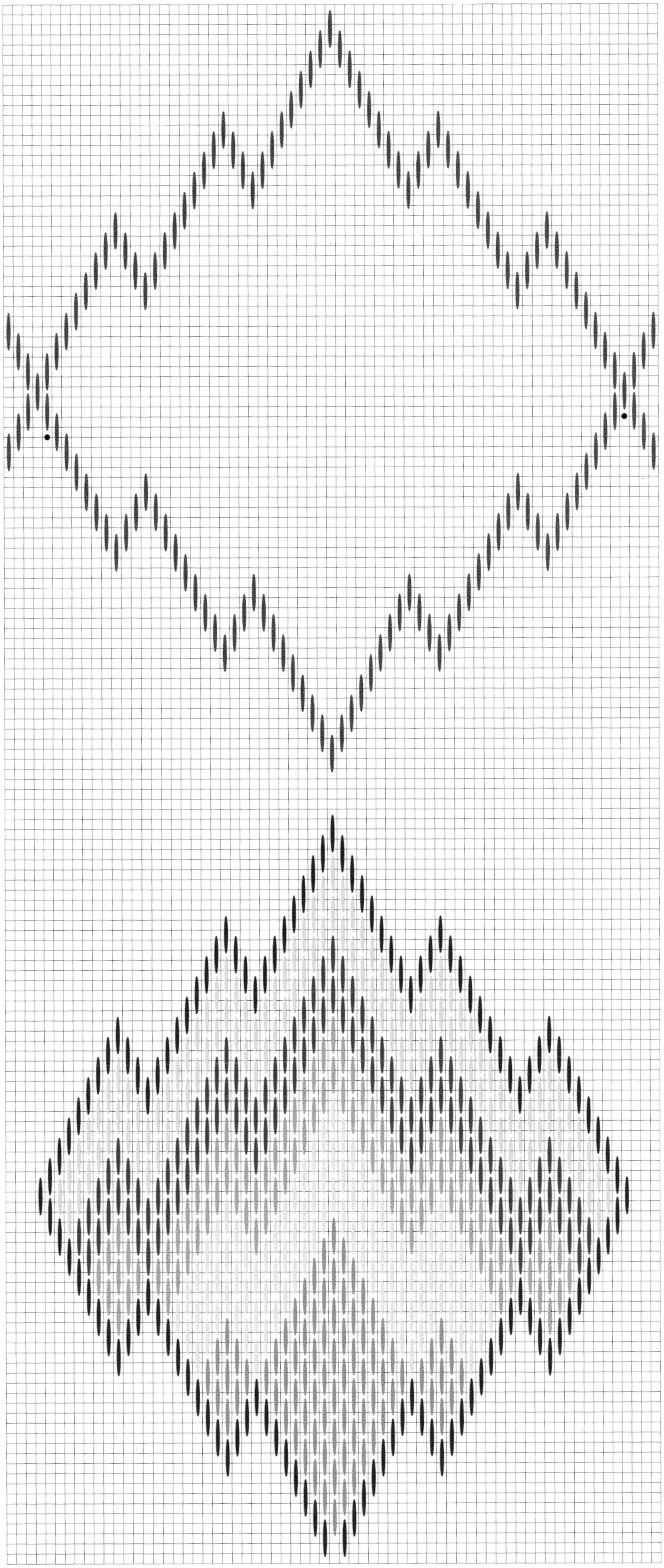

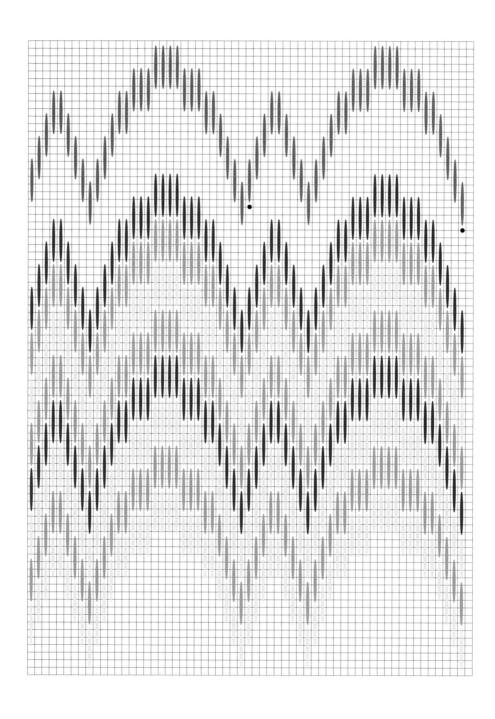

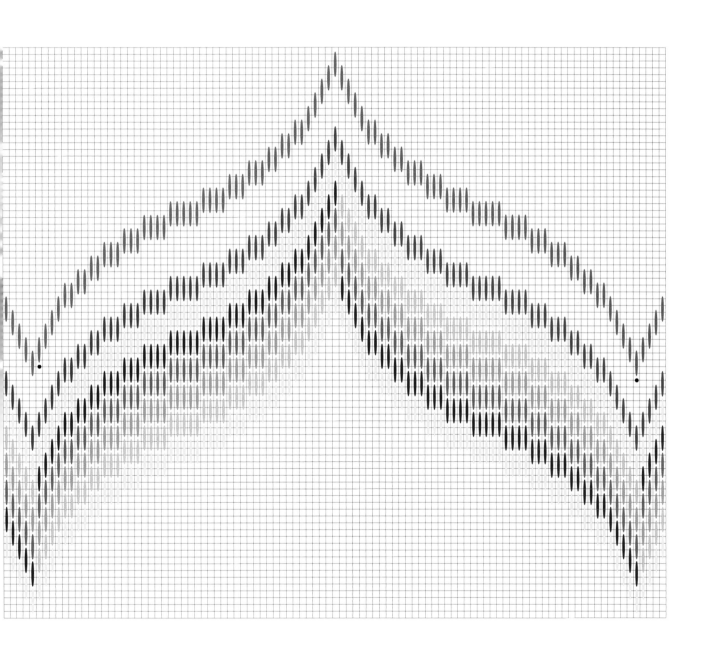

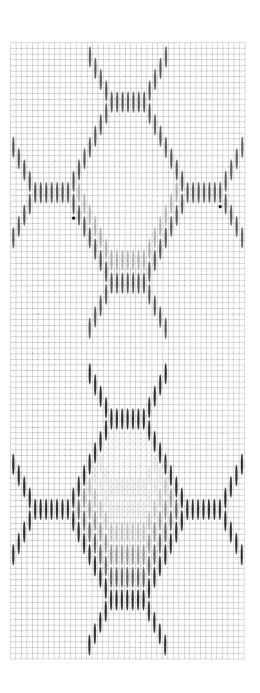

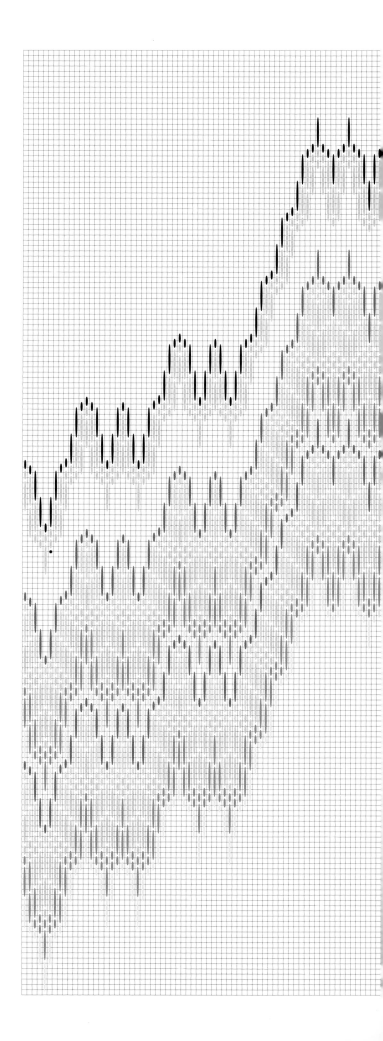

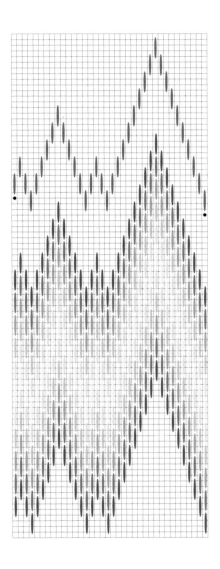

Bibliography

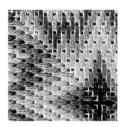

BOOKS ON
EMBROIDERY AND
NEEDLEWORK
Billcliffe, Roger,
Mackintosh Textile Designs
(London: Fine Art Society/New
York: Taplinger, 1982)

Clabburn, Pamela,
Needleworker's Dictionary
(London: Macmillan, 1976)

Field, Peggy, and Linsley, June,
Canvas Embroidery
(London: Merehurst, 1990)

Gostelow, Mary,
*Embroidery: Traditional Techniques
and Patterns from all over the
World* (London: Cavendish House,
1977)

Hughes, Therle,
*English Domestic Needlework,
1660–1860*
(London: Lutterworth/New York:
Macmillan, 1961)

Kennet, Frances, and Scarlett,
Belinda,
Country House Needlepoint
(London: Conran Octopus, 1988)

Muller, Barbara,
*Florentine Embroidery: All you
Need to Know for Perfect Results*
(Wellingborough, Northants.:
Thorson, 1989; first pub. in
German, 1986)

Peri, Paolo,
Tessuti barocchi al Bargello
(Florence: SPES/Museo Nazionale
del Bargello, 1997)

Rhodes, Mary,
*Needlepoint: The Art of Canvas
Embroidery* (London: Cathay
Books, 1974)

Thomas, Mary,
*Mary Thomas's Dictionary of
Embroidery Stitches* (London:
Hodder & Stoughton, 1934)

Windrum, Sarah,
*Needlepoint: Over 20 New and
Original Projects for you to Make*
(London: Octopus, 1980)

*Zigzag Stitchery: 50 New and
Colourful Looks in Florentine
Embroidery* (London: Marshall
Cavendish, 1972)

SOURCES OF DESIGN
INSPIRATION
Blossfeldt, Karl,
Art Forms in Nature
(London: Zwemmer, 1936)

Clarke, Ethne,
*Leaf, Bark and Berry: Foliage Plants
for Texture and Form*
(Newton Abbot, Devon: David &
Charles, 1996)

Ferguson, Henry, and Procter,
Lynn,
The Art of the Tattoo (London:
Greenwich Editions/ Pennsylvania:
Courage Books, 1998)

Foods that Harm, Foods that Heal
(London: Reader's Digest, 1996)

*Japanese Ornament: From the
17th to the 19th Century*
(Ware, Herts.: Wordsworth
Editions, 1991)

Riley, Noel, *Tile Art* (London:
Apple Press, 1987)

Slesin, Suzanne, et al.,
Japanese Style
(New York and London:
Thames & Hudson, 1987)

Spring, Christopher,
African Textiles
(London: Bracken, 1989)

Stuart, David,
Gardening with Antique Plants
(London: Conran Octopus, 1997)

Tunnicliffe, C. F.,
A Sketchbook of Birds
(London: Victor Gollancz, 1979)

Tutino Vercelloni, Isa,
*Missonologia: The World of
Missoni* (Cologne: Taschen/
New York: Abbeville Press, 1995)

Warren, Geoffrey, and Klein, Dan
Art Nouveau and Art Deco
(London: Galley Press, 1978)

Suppliers

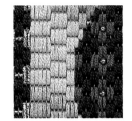

UNITED KINGDOM

DMC Creative World Ltd
Pullman Road
Wigston
Leicestershire LE18 2DY
(DMC threads, DMC beads,
Zweigart canvas)

Framecraft Miniatures Ltd
372/376 Summer Lane
Hockley
Birmingham B19 3QA
(Wooden box, Mill Hill beads)

Macleod Craft Marketing
West Yonderton
Warlock Road
Bridge of Weir
Renfrewshire PA11 3SR
(Caron threads)

Christine Kingdom
Creative Marketing Services
57 Kiln Ride
Wokingham
Berkshire RG40 3PJ
(Offray ribbon)

Mary Jane Collection
Tir-y-Fron Lane
Pontybodkin
Mold
Denbighshire CH7 4TU
(YLI Silk Ribbon)

Coats Crafts UK
PO Box 22
The Lingfield Estate
McMullen Road
Darlington
Co. Durham DL1 1YQ
(Anchor threads, crochet
cotton, Kreinik metallic
threads)

Willow Fabrics
95 Town Lane
Mobberly
Cheshire WA16 7HH
(Zweigart canvas, Zweigart
Davosa)

The Craft Collection
Terry Mills
Westfield Road
Horbury
Wakefield
West Yorkshire WF4 6HD
(Paterna wool)

UNITED STATES
OF AMERICA

DMC Corp.
Port Kearny
Building 10
South Kearny, NJ 07032
(DMC threads, beads)

Joan Toggit Ltd
2 Riverside Drive
Somerset, NJ 07032
(Zweigart canvas, Zweigart
Davosa)

The Caron Collection
67 Poland Street
Bridgeport CT 06605
(Caron threads)

C. M. Offray & Son Ltd
Route 24
Box 601
Chester, NJ 07930–0601
(satin ribbons)

Sudbery House
Colton Road
Box 895
Old Lyme, CT 0637
(Wooden box)

Gay Bowles Sales, Inc.
PO Box 1060
Jamesville, WI 53547–1060
(Mill Hill beads)

YLI Corp.
161 West Main Street
Rock Hill, SC 29730
(silk ribbon)

Kreinik
3106 Lord Baltimore Drive
101
Baltimore, MD 21244
(Kreinik metallic threads)

Coats & Clark
4135 South Boulevard
Charlotte, NC 28217
(Coats threads)

Thread colour conversion tables

Please note that these tables should be used only as a guide, since exact equivalents are not always available. Only colours used in the projects in this book are listed here, and the information is not necessarily endorsed by the manufacturers. Internet users will find other tables available on manufacturers' and enthusiasts' websites; these will not always agree with one another, because some subjective judgement is involved in matching colours.

Stranded cottons, Anchor to DMC

Anchor	DMC	Anchor	DMC	Anchor	DMC
01	blanc	150	823	883	3064
23	963	161	518	884	920
55	603	167	3761	886	677
57	602	189	3812	888	3828
90	3727	213	369	920	932
98	553	214	368	1011	948
100	552	215	320	1030	3746
108	210	216	562	1031	3753
109	209	217	319	1032	3752
112	3837	227	701	1033	932
118	340	246	986	1034	931
119	333	253	772	1036	3750
120	3747	254	472	1038	519
121	794	255	907	1045	436
123	791	256	906	1050	3781
129	3325	258	905	1060	828
142	798	274	928	1062	598
		307	3852	1064	597
		309	782	1066	3810
		326	720	1089	996
		336	758	1092	964
		341	919	9159	828
		342	211		
		361	738		
		844	3012		
		846	936		
		853	372		
		859	3053		
		869	3743		
		870	3042		
		871	3041		
		873	3740		
		875	3817		
		881	945		
		882	758		

Anchor	DMC
738	942
739	852
758	868
807	168
922	1003
3750	1036
3756	1037
3766	168
3768	840
3802	no match
3808	66
3809	85
3810	1064
3811	1060

Stranded cottons, DMC to Anchor

DMC	Anchor
150	59
152	894
154	no match
356	5975
436	1045
500	683
503	876 (approx.)
720	326
722	323

Tapestry wools, Anchor to DMC

Anchor	DMC
8440	7107
8488	no match
8550	7015
8552	7016
8808	7037
8902	7926
8904	7339
8914	7599
8918	7598
9800	noir

ABOUT THE AUTHOR

Brenda Day was born in the north-west of England. She trained as an embroideress at Bromley College of Art and then at Manchester College of Art. During her initial years as a teacher she undertook design work for the Needlework Development Scheme and completed various commissions for Lancashire Education Committee.

A move to Wales, where her children were born and where she still lives, coincided with an award from the Design Council. In 1988 she set up a company to design and produce embroidery kits for the Welsh tourist market, inspired by Celtic and Welsh art and history. Brenda also works as a freelance designer for a variety of companies, including some national magazines. She has had two books on embroidery published; this is her third.

Index

GMC Publications

BOOKS

CRAFTS

American Patchwork Designs in Needlepoint	Melanie Tacon
Bargello: A Fresh Approach to Florentine Embroidery	Brenda Day
Beginning Picture Marquetry	Lawrence Threadgold
Blackwork: A New Approach	Brenda Day
Celtic Cross Stitch Designs	Carol Phillipson
Celtic Knotwork Designs	Sheila Sturrock
Celtic Knotwork Handbook	Sheila Sturrock
Celtic Spirals and Other Designs	Sheila Sturrock
Complete Pyrography	Stephen Poole
Creating Made-to-Measure Knitwear: A Revolutionary Approach to Knitwear Design	Sylvia Wynn
Creative Backstitch	Helen Hall
Creative Embroidery Techniques Using Colour Through Gold	Daphne J. Ashby & Jackie Woolsey
The Creative Quilter: Techniques and Projects	Pauline Brown
Cross-Stitch Designs from China	Carol Phillipson
Decoration on Fabric: A Sourcebook of Ideas	Pauline Brown
Decorative Beaded Purses	Enid Taylor
Designing and Making Cards	Glennis Gilruth
Glass Engraving Pattern Book	John Everett
Glass Painting	Emma Sedman
Handcrafted Rugs	Sandra Hardy
How to Arrange Flowers: A Japanese Approach to English Design	Taeko Marvelly
How to Make First-Class Cards	Debbie Brown
An Introduction to Crewel Embroidery	Mave Glenny
Making and Using Working Drawings for Realistic Model Animals	Basil F. Fordham
Making Character Bears	Valerie Tyler
Making Decorative Screens	Amanda Howes
Making Fabergé-Style Eggs	Denise Hopper
Making Fairies and Fantastical Creatures	Julie Sharp
Making Greetings Cards for Beginners	Pat Sutherland
Making Hand-Sewn Boxes: Techniques and Projects	Jackie Woolsey
Making Mini Cards, Gift Tags & Invitations	Glennis Gilruth
Making Soft-Bodied Dough Characters	Patricia Hughes
Natural Ideas for Christmas: Fantastic Decorations to Make	Josie Cameron-Ashcroft & Carol Cox
New Ideas for Crochet: Stylish Projects for the Home	Darsha Capaldi
Papercraft Projects for Special Occasions	Sine Chesterman
Patchwork for Beginners	Pauline Brown
Pyrography Designs	Norma Gregory
Pyrography Handbook (Practical Crafts)	Stephen Poole
Rose Windows for Quilters	Angela Besley
Rubber Stamping with Other Crafts	Lynne Garner
Silk Painting	Jill Clay
Sponge Painting	Ann Rooney
Stained Glass: Techniques and Projects	Mary Shanahan

Step-by-Step Pyrography Projects for the Solid Point Machine	Norma Gregory
Tassel Making for Beginners	Enid Taylor
Tatting Collage	Lindsay Rogers
Tatting Patterns	Lyn Morton
Temari: A Traditional Japanese Embroidery Technique	Margaret Ludlow
Trip Around the World: 25 Patchwork, Quilting and Appliqué Projects	Gail Lawther
Trompe l'Oeil: Techniques and Projects	Jan Lee Johnson
Tudor Treasures to Embroider	Pamela Warner
Wax Art	Hazel Marsh

UPHOLSTERY

The Upholsterer's Pocket Reference Book	David James
Upholstery: A Complete Course (Revised Edition)	David James
Upholstery Restoration	David James
Upholstery Techniques & Projects	David James
Upholstery Tips and Hints	David James

TOYMAKING

Scrollsaw Toy Projects	Ivor Carlyle
Scrollsaw Toys for All Ages	Ivor Carlyle

DOLLS' HOUSES AND MINIATURES

1/12 Scale Character Figures for the Dolls' House	James Carrington
Americana in 1/12 Scale: 50 Authentic Projects	Joanne Ogreenc & Mary Lou Santovec
Architecture for Dolls' Houses	Joyce Percival
The Authentic Georgian Dolls' House	Brian Long
A Beginners' Guide to the Dolls' House Hobby	Jean Nisbett
Celtic, Medieval and Tudor Wall Hangings in 1/12 Scale Needlepoint	Sandra Whitehead
Creating Decorative Fabrics: Projects in 1/12 Scale	Janet Storey
The Dolls' House 1/24 Scale: A Complete Introduction	Jean Nisbett
Dolls' House Accessories, Fixtures and Fittings	Andrea Barham
Dolls' House Furniture: Easy-to-Make Projects in 1/12 Scale	Freida Gray
Dolls' House Makeovers	Jean Nisbett
Dolls' House Window Treatments	Eve Harwood
Easy to Make Dolls' House Accessories	Andrea Barham
Edwardian-Style Hand-Knitted Fashion for 1/12 Scale Dolls	Yvonne Wakefield
How to Make Your Dolls' House Special: Fresh Ideas for Decorating	Beryl Armstrong
Make Your Own Dolls' House Furniture	Maurice Harper
Making Dolls' House Furniture	Patricia King
Making Georgian Dolls' Houses	Derek Rowbottom
Making Miniature Chinese Rugs and Carpets	Carol Phillipson
Making Miniature Food and Market Stalls	Angie Scarr
Making Miniature Gardens	Freida Gray

WOODWORKING

VIDEOS

MAGAZINES

WOODTURNING • WOODCARVING • FURNITURE & CABINETMAKING • THE ROUTER
NEW WOODWORKING • THE DOLLS' HOUSE MAGAZINE • OUTDOOR PHOTOGRAPHY • BLACK &
WHITE PHOTOGRAPHY • TRAVEL PHOTOGRAPHY • MACHINE KNITTING NEWS • BusinessMatters

The above represents a full list of all titles currently published or scheduled to be published. All are available direct from the Publishers or through bookshops, newsagents and specialist retailers. To place an order, or to obtain a complete catalogue, contact:

GMC Publications,
Castle Place, 166 High Street, Lewes, East Sussex BN7 1XU, United Kingdom
Tel: 01273 488005 Fax: 01273 478606   E-mail: pubs@thegmcgroup.com

Orders by credit card are accepted